Library of Congress: 95-81081
ISBN: 0-9649489-0-7
Printed in the United States of America
Cover Design & Book Production
Pamela Carrasco

REVOLUTION DESIGN

Dedication
To my daughters, Christine, Nancy and Sarah Rose

Acknowledgements
With special thanks to Laura Gasparis Vonfrolio, RN whose encouragement and support helped to make this book possible and to Pamela Carrasco for her layout design.

About The Author

George Stern, Jr. has served on the management faculty of the City University of New York's College of Staten Island for over 25 years. His expertise in the areas of Management, Team Building, Motivation, Communication and Organizational Change has enabled him to help thousands of individuals to increase their personal productivity, job satisfaction and happiness.

He serves as a Performance Consultant to various businesses. He conducts Professional Development Seminars and Workshops and consistently receives rave reviews from participants. His programs provide a wide range of resources for business, nonprofit, government and educational organizations.

He is a much sought after speaker and is characterized as being a Creative, Dynamic and Enthusiastic individual who makes learning FUN.

To find out more information about his Professional Development Programs, Seminars, and/or Speaking Engagements, please call or write to:

Ms. Phyllis Neary
72 Granger Dr.
Feeding Hills, MA 01030-1624

The AHP Group
George Stern, Jr.
P.O. Box 70206
Staten Island, NY 10307
(888) 817-4961
FAX: (718) 227-5293

TABLE OF CONTENTS

Introduction

Well, here it is! Just what the world needs, another book. Why in the sea of books on the market, should there be another one? Good question.

In today's rapidly changing, high-tech society, it has become easy for people to become overwhelmed with the accelerating rate of change and the growing volume of "information" made available to them.

Many people seem frustrated and confused by a growing feeling of not being able to keep up with all that is happening around them. From parenting, to corporate down-sizing; from societal values to educational shortcomings; from health issues to environmental issues; people seem to be limited in their options about how to deal with these changes.

This book is a kind of 'TIME OUT' period. It is an opportunity for you to get some fresh insights, or maybe to 're-fresh' some old insights, so you can better positively manage some of those everyday challenges that life throws your way.

It will help you better focus on what's really important in your life. It will give you ideas that you can use to help make your life a little less stressful and happier,

> *"A book must be the axe for the frozen sea inside us."*
> *-Kafka*

and give you some laughs from time to time.

I do not come to you as an expert. In today's world of rapid change, experts have a short life-span. I come to you as a 'student' journeying thorough life. In writing this book, I have found myself coming up with more questions than answers. So often in life, it is the questions that begin any journey. This book is intended to serve as a reference tool for your journey, where ever you desire to go.

Publishers' statistics suggest that less than 1% of all books purchased are actually read cover to cover. This book may be no exception. In order for you to benefit from reading it, you will not have to read it cover to cover(although I hope you do).

To get the most from this book, my first suggestion is that you don't think of it as a 'book.' This might seem a strange request, but let me explain. Most people when they think of a 'book,' think of it as something to read. Well, reading alone can give you information, and while information can be helpful, it alone, will not improve the quality of your life. ACTION is the key to growth in life. The world is full of people who have knowledge. If knowledge and information where the keys to happiness and success in life, then anyone with an

> *"Information will not change your life. Action will."*

education would be happy and successful. We all know that's not true.

To get the most from your reading, I would like you to think of it as a 'tool' rather than a book. A 'tool' is something you use to achieve or accomplish a particular result. Usually, it is something you use over and over, whenever a particular result is desired. This 'tool' is designed to be used in that way. You will notice it has wide margins so it is easier to read. You can also use the extra page space to make helpful notes and comments for yourself. The print is a bit larger and the sentences and paragraphs are presented in a style that makes it easier to use.

The most important aspect, is not what is written in this 'tool,' but rather what impact the ideas presented have on your own thinking. The thoughts and feelings that are triggered by what you experience as you travel through this 'tool' will be most important for you. As you take note of your thoughts and feelings, the ideas become yours.

As much as I would like to claim that the ideas presented in this 'tool' are mine alone, I cannot. They are combinations of the ideas of countless other thinkers. They are compilations of thousands of written works and experiences. All the wisdom of the ages is contained in books. Since the

"The real purpose of books is to trap the mind into doing its own thinking."
-Christopher Morley

beginning of time, people have worked to record their thinking so that it can be preserved throughout history. This 'tool' represents my attempt to do the same. I have taken from my experiences, and added my own perspectives.

This 'tool' has been structured to amuse you at times and to challenge your thinking at other times. You are your own mentor on this journey. You will be asking yourself many questions as you journey through this 'tool'. You will find that thinking, in one sense, is really nothing more than a process of asking and answering questions. The better questions you ask yourself, the better thinking you will generate.

Real, meaningful learning involves asking YOUR own questions. These are the questions that have the most meaning to you. I will be asking you questions as you go along to help stimulate your thinking.

Well, it's time to begin your journey. You won't need to take your American Express card with you, just an open and alert mind and a desire to learn and have some fun. Good luck! Let's get started.

Beliefs Can Create Reality

Roger Bannister was the first person to run a mile under four minutes. Before he did, experts believed that the human body could not run at that speed.

In the fifteenth century, it was the widespread belief that the earth was flat. Columbus obviously did not support that belief.

When John F. Kennedy, committed us to landing a man on the moon, it was believed by many, that this could not be accomplished in our lifetime.

Whether you realize it or not, "beliefs" are very powerful forces in your daily life. But, what are they?

Very simply, a belief is nothing more than a feeling of certainty you have about something. You can believe that the Yankees are going to be in the World Series, or that vanilla ice cream is the best ice cream in the world. You can also believe that you cannot lose weight or get the kind of job you really want.

These are really simple ideas and you might even say that they are opinions rather than beliefs. You see, often, what

A belief is nothing more than a feeling of certainty you have about something.

1

you feel is a belief may in effect be just an opinion.

Most people go through life without really challenging their beliefs. They simply feel that since it is their belief, it has to be true.

Whether a belief is true or false is not the issue. What is most important is whether the belief is helpful to you. Does it empower you, put you in a resourceful state or, does it disempower you, put you in an unproductive state? For example, how old were you before you realized that you could tear off those tags on your pillows without going to jail (be honest now). You remember, those little tags with the terrifying messages, "do not remove under penalty of law." Your parents probably warned you not to touch those things.

Many people travel through life, carrying beliefs about themselves and others that are totally unresourceful. These beliefs may have developed from family, educators, society, the media, friends, and the list goes on.

The point is, your family may have been well intentioned when they told you what you could do in life. Your teachers may have been well intentioned when they told you what you should or shouldn't do with your career. But the

" Whether you believe you can do a thing or not, you are right. "
-Henry Ford

real fact is that YOU have the ultimate power over your life.

Society is continually placing limits on people's potential. That is why beliefs need to be continually challenged. Too often, an individual goes through life with a belief they feel is true, when in reality, it is a self-limiting "opinion" they have about themselves.

If Roger Bannister had accepted the beliefs and opinions of "experts," he could not have broken the four minute mile.

Beliefs need to be continually challenged and not accepted as blind truth.

The world is full of people who will tell you what you can't do. Just think about people who have achieved what initially seemed impossible. People like Gandhi, George Washington, Winston Churchill, Mother Teresa, Bob Weiland (an amputee who lost both legs in Vietnam and runs marathons on his hands), Martin Luther King, etc.

These people achieved great feats. But what about you? What would you like to accomplish? What's been holding you back? What beliefs are you living with that may be limiting you? Why not challenge them? Read about people who have accomplished great things. Find out what kind of beliefs they had and

3

how they handled adversity.

Your goal doesn't have to be earth shaking. Maybe you just want to lose weight or go back to school. Whatever you want to do, begin to challenge some of your beliefs that have prevented you from accomplishing what you want. Remember, the important thing is not whether your beliefs are true or false, but whether they put you in a resourceful or and unresourceful state. Do they encourage you?

Beliefs are very powerful. In the words of Henry Ford, "Whether you believe you can do a thing or not, you are right." What do you think?

How Much Of Your Brain Are You Using?

If some one asked you if you were left handed or right handed, that would not be difficult to answer. But, what if they asked if you were right brained or left brained? That question may be a little more challenging to answer.

In the late 1960s and early 1970s, the work of Roger Sperry and Robert Ornstein relating to the human brain, won them a Nobel Prize. In brief, their work discovered that our brain has two sides or cortices. For most people, the left side functions in the areas of reasoning, words, logic, numbers and analysis. The right side is more concerned with things like imagination, images, rhythms, color and pattern recognition.

Our educational system is dominated by left-brain oriented activities.

Now, in addition to these discoveries, further research suggested that many people tend to develop or use one side of their brain more than the other. It can be argued that we live in a left-brain oriented world of numbers, logic and reasoning. Our educational system is dominated by left-brain oriented activities. So, it is not surprising that for many people, their thinking is dominated by left-brain operations.

5

As a result of this, for many people, the right brain activities lie underdeveloped. When people describe themselves as talented in certain ways, they tend to focus on those areas that they have developed and ignore those that they have not. For example, too few people think of themselves as creative, which tends to be a right brain oriented function. In most instances, it is not that they are not creative but rather that they have tended to use more of their left brain than their right. Their creativity is in a kind of dormant state simply because it is not being utilized.

If you are right handed, you will tend to use your right hand much more often than your left. But, if you began to use your left hand more, you would strengthen your ability to use both. One of the interesting research findings about the brain is that if you work at developing the part of your brain that is underdeveloped, it has a synergistic affect on your whole brain. That is, by working to strengthen your weaker side, you will get the benefit of strengthening both sides at the same time.

What brain research is finding is that in order to better use our brains, we need to learn to develop both sides. Remember, brain research is a relatively new area. Most of what we have discovered about

Scientists,

conducting brain

research, suggest

that the

average person

is only using

1/10 of 1%

of their

brain's capabilities

the brain is only about 30 years old.

The most highly developed, advanced learning model we have is the human baby. If you think about it, by the time most children are two years old, they can speak. This is something we take for granted. But just consider all the learning activities they have to go through to be able to do this. Consider all the activities you would have to go through if you had to learn a new language. A baby exemplifies how both sides of the brain, working and being developed together, can synergistically be used to maximize learning.

In order for a baby to learn a language, it must be able to control and understand such things as: music, linguistics, memory, creativity, logic, pattern recognition, thinking, imaging, physics, and mathematics, to name a few. Is there any doubt, that we human beings greatly underestimate the capabilities of our brains?

If scientists conducting brain research suggest that the average person is only using 1/10 of 1% of their brain's capabilities, perhaps we should seek out some brain manuals. Isn't it ironic that we have manuals for just about everything we own; cars, VCRs, vacuum

7

cleaners, microwaves, cameras, watches, computers, and the list goes on. What about a brain manual? Would you buy one? Would you use it if you had one? What about in school? Shouldn't schools be the places where brain research findings should be used? Do you think that brain research is uncovering more effective ways of learning?

If babies can be viewed as the most extraordinary, intellectually advanced, learning beings, what happens to us on our way to adulthood? Why do our younger years have to be the most powerful time in our learning cycle? With only 1/10 of 1% of our brain's capacity being utilized there have got to be more powerful ways to learn. Could it be that as we get older, we think too much and that our thinking may be of a nature that actually restricts our ability to learn? What do you think?

The Changeless Nature Of Change

Comfort brings with it a sense of predictability.

It is happening as you are reading this. It comes from out of nowhere. No one or no thing can escape its grasp. It affects the living and the dead. And, you are powerless to stop it. You can attempt to fight it. You can deny its existence. And, most of the time, you are not even aware its happening, until it's too late. What is it? It is the universal constant, it is change and it is never ending.

At no time, in the history of the world, have we humans been so impacted by the rapid, and accelerating rate of change. It is all around us. How do you react to change?

Far too many people view change in negative, disempowering ways. To these people, change is viewed as a threat. People have a strong desire to be comfortable. Comfort brings with it a sense of predictability. Most of us like to know what to expect as we move into the future. We have, through our past habits, developed certain, zones of comfort. While comforting, they can also insulate us from new, and improved ways of doing things.

9

Because of the rapid rates of change, in many areas of life, people have been forced, kicking and screaming, out of their zones of comfort. As we look around the world today, we find confusion and uncertainty. The old ways of doing things have changed. The old ways of thinking have changed.

People living in the countries that formally made up the Soviet Union, are being challenged with the dramatic change of being FREE. We are living in the age of the ENTREPRENEUR. Economic growth is not coming from the old industrial giants like General Motors, General Electric and Sears, but from industries and companies that weren't around ten years ago.

We are seeing our educational philosophy being challenged. Our political system and the thinking of politicians have just received a major wake up call. Political thinking of the past is being challenged, not just here, but throughout the world. In the areas of computers, communication, health care, management and the sciences, change is the operative word. The population movement away from the big northern cities to the south and the west is a result of some of these changes, and it will continue.

"Tomorrow's illiterate will not be the man who can't read; he will be the man who has not learned how to learn."
-Alvin Toffler

These are all healthy developments. These changes need to be viewed positively, and as opportunities for new growth and learning. If we refuse to embrace change; if we insist on doing things the old way; we will only short-circuit our success, excitement and happiness in life.

One of the most important and most powerful skills for the 21st century will be the skill of learning how to learn. Alvin Toffler captures this idea so well when he states in his book, Future Shock, that, "Tomorrow's illiterate will not be the man who can't read; he will be the man who has not learned how to learn."

Change brings with it many opportunities. But, it also demands that we learn. Those who refuse to move out of the comfort zones of ignorance, will find themselves in a world of confusion, uncertainty and fear. Those who risk becoming uncomfortable; those who risk the challenges that meaningful learning requires; those that embrace change for its opportunities; they are the ones who will reap the rewards of success, happiness and growth.

Each of us, regardless of our age or our position, should regularly examine our own individual thinking and behavior to determine where we can change and provide more growth and challenge in our own careers and lives. In the words of Marie Curie, "Nothing in life is to be feared. It is only to be understood." What do you think?

"Nothing in life is to be feared. It is only to be understood."
-Marie Curie

The MINDBODY Effect

Dr. Deepak Chopra M.D., is one of the world's top endocrinologists (a specialist on how hormones affect the body). He is the best selling author of such books as: "Quantum Healing", "Perfect Health" and "Ageless Body, Timeless Mind". Because he continues to challenge a number of accepted beliefs about the relationships between the mind, the body, health and wellness, some of his thinking has proven to be controversial within the medical profession. He has been characterized as being "a pioneer in the medicine of the future." The following, represent some of Chopra's ideas. They are presented to stimulate your thinking and are not intended to serve as proven and accepted medical facts.

Chopra, and others, believe that the mind exists in every cell of the body. Rather than having a mind and a body, we have a kind of MINDBODY. It has been suggested that the human body has more chemical reactions occurring in it in one day then all the chemical plants in the world.

One of the contributors to these chemical reactions are thoughts. A thought, is an impulse of information and energy that triggers a chemical reaction in our body. Chopra believes that the average person has about 60,000 thoughts per day. That's

The average person has about 60,000 thoughts per day.

-Deepak Chopra

13

the good news. The bad news is that 95% of these are the same thoughts of the previous day.

To Chopra's thinking, we can't have a thought without our immune system knowing about it. Our immune system is actually a thinking system within a floating nervous system. This belief is not unique to Chopra. Dr. Herbert Benson of the Harvard Medical School expressed a similar view in his 1979 classic best seller, "The Mind/Body Effect".

Our bodies are considered to be our own unique pharmacies.

Our bodies are considered to be our own unique pharmacies. They are capable of producing whatever drugs we need, whenever we need them, and in whatever dosages we need. And, very importantly, they are able to deliver these drugs to the exact location and in the right dosage when they are needed. This eliminates the side effects that are often created when drugs are delivered from outside the body. Illness and disease occur when our body's ability to do this breaks down.

Through the use of increasingly more sophisticated technology, we are becoming more skilled at being able to better understand the connection between the mind and body and how this connection impacts wellness, illness and disease.

14

One of Chopra's beliefs is that our interpretation of reality can cause our mindbody to produce drugs. These drugs can have either a positive or negative affect on the body. The challenge we face is that in assessing reality, we are very often limited by our five senses.

In Chopra's mind, the average person is only capable of processing about one-billionth of what is going on around them at any given moment. Think about this for a moment, only one-billionth! For example, while you are reading this, how aware are you of the millions of activities that are going on within your body at this very instant?

Consider the input our senses suggest about the earth. Based solely on our sensual input, it is very easy to perceive the earth as being flat, stationary and solid. This was the world view through the fifteenth century. Most people will acknowledge today, that the earth is neither flat nor stationary. But, most would have a more difficult time accepting the idea that it is not solid.

In understanding that the earth is not solid, it is necessary to go beyond our senses and to enter the world of Quantum Physics. In this world, we travel beyond the limitations of our senses. The world here is viewed as one composed atomic and sub-atomic particles. By dic-

Our bodies are in effect, 99.999% empty space.

tionary definition, an atom is empty space. From this definition, since all matter is composed of atoms, all matter, in a quantum physical sense, can be interpreted as being empty space. What appears to our senses as being solid matter, in reality, is merely empty space. How would this be for a topic at your next barbecue?

From this perspective, Chopra explains that our bodies are in effect, 99.999% empty space. He begins to look at illness, disease and wellness from a different perspective. He characterizes our bodies as being a constant stream of low energy flow. Illness and disease can be explained as factors that restrict and interrupt this flow of energy.

If you have read this far, your experience has been a little like Star Trek's Starship Enterprise, taking you to places you haven't gone before. But, as we accelerate our ability to uncover new knowledge and understanding through sophisticated technology, we also find ourselves challenging not only our accepted beliefs about nature and our world, but also exploring areas where no one has gone before.

This is what makes the future so exciting. And, it is also what makes some of Chopra's beliefs so stimulating and at the same time threatening and controversial. His thinking, as well as the thinking of others, is challenging us to look at the mind, the body, wellness, health, illness and disease in new and different ways. What do you think?

Is It Whack
Time Yet?

When was the last time you got a good whack? According to creativity consultant Roger Von Oech, a whack is anything that causes you to think differently. To Von Oech, whacks come in all shapes and sizes. A whack can be a problem, a failure, a joke, a surprise, an accident, a divorce, a question, anything that gets you to think differently. The question becomes, "Do you generate your own whacks or do you allow yourself to be whacked by outside circumstances?"

Von Oech believes that whacks are stimulants for creativity. The unfortunate fact is that far too many people believe that they are not very creative. In actuality, everyone has creative potential, but too few work to turn that potential into reality. Creativity is a skill and like any skill it needs to be developed.

It is easy for people to recognize the need for creativity in music, literature and the arts in general. But, how about the need for creativity in everyday life? What prevents people from becoming more creative at work, at home and at play? It's their rules and their routines. Without giving it much thought, we all have developed rules and routines for getting through our

Creativity is a skill and like any skill it needs to be developed.

day-to-day experiences. The more rules and routines we have, the less we have to think.

Just think about all the routines you have during the course of the day that require little or no creative thought. How much thought goes into your normal morning routine, to the route you take to work, to the routine you have when you get to work, etc.? Now don't get me wrong, we need rules and routines in order to get things done. But, the more rules and routines we have, the more frustration and confusion we will experience when conditions in our external environment change.

For many people, their rules and routines are whacked for them by external factors. These are factors that they have no control over. When this happens, people seek to find the right solution to a given situation. Von Oech believes that it is this seeking of the right solution that can stifle our creativity. He states in his book, "A Whack On The Side Of The Head," that much of our educational system is structured to teach people the right answer. For the average person who finishes college, he or she will have taken over 2,600 quizzes, tests and exams most of which served to ingrain the concept of the right

...one technique for stimulating your creativity is to ask different questions.

18

answer in people's thinking. While this may be good for mathematical situations, most of life doesn't present itself in right answer form. In life, there are many right answers, depending on what you look for. When you think there is only one right answer, you stop looking. A noted educator, Neil Postman has observed that, "Children enter school as question marks and leave as periods."

Von Oech suggests that one technique for stimulating your creativity is to ask different questions. By asking questions like, "What are the right answers to this situation?" and/or "What are the meanings of this?" you open your mind to more than one possibility.

Another creativity technique is to vary your routines and rules. Take a different route to work in the morning. Read a different newspaper or magazine. Go for a walk at lunch time. Get up an hour earlier in the morning. Remember, the more you stay in your routines, the less opportunity you will have to be creative. What do you think?

Neil Postman has observed that, "Children enter school as question marks and leave as periods."

Creating Moments

It had been a particularly challenging day at work and she was tired. As she opened the door of her apartment, she was embraced by the aroma of flowers. When she turned on the lights, she saw flowers in the kitchen, the living room, the bathroom and the bedrooms. Each floral grouping, and she counted thirty of them, had a little note which read, "Because I Love You." It wasn't her birthday. It wasn't her anniversary. It was just a Thursday. But, it was a Thursday she would never forget, thanks to her husband.

With all the days you have experienced in your life, how many brought with them an experience so unique and so enjoyable, you will never forget them? I'd bet your answer would be a mere handful.

If you are 30 years old, you have lived through approximately 10,960 days. If you 60, you have about 21,900 days in your life bank.

Most of us go through each day with a certain set of expectations. To a large degree, we have little control over what happens around us and to us each day. Sure, we can plan our day, or at least attempt to plan our day, but life usually has

If you are 30 years old, you have lived through approximately 10,960 days.

a way of following a different daily plan more often than not.

With these ideas in mind, there is a power that everyone has, but it is a power very few people really use. The reason this power isn't used frequently is because most people don't realize they have it. What is this power you ask? It is the power to create for someone, a memory that is so unique and so special, they will never forget it.

Too many people go through life vastly underestimating their powers and abilities.

Imagine the magnitude of this power. With all the thousands of days in a person's life, you have the power to create for them, an experience so out of the ordinary, so out of the routine of their daily life, it will live in their memory forever. What a power!

One of the great things about this power is that you can use it at any age. You are never too old to use it. It is a power that is limitless. The only thing that limits this power is your creativity and innovation. Each of these is without boundaries.

Another exciting aspect of this power to create moments is that it is not limited to just individuals. It is not limited to people you know. You can use it to create moments for a stranger, for families, for organizations, for teams, for schools, for classes, and the list can go on and on.

What limits the use of this power is a person's lack of awareness that he or she has it. Once this limitation is overcome, the challenge becomes creatively seeking opportunities to use it. This is the fun part. Too many people go through life vastly underestimating their powers and abilities. By becoming more aware of the powers you have to positively impact the life and the memory of others, you strengthen your powers to improve the quality of life. What do you think?

The Cheapest Commodity On Earth

The

world

is full

of

critics.

What do you think is the cheapest commodity on earth? It would have to be something that is in abundant supply and at the same time has very little demand. If you answered, criticism, you are right.

How often do you go out looking for it? Do you ever lie awake at night worrying that you may not get enough criticism next week? I don't think so. In fact, I would speculate that you are probably getting too much criticism.

The world is full of critics. It doesn't take much to be one. All you need, in most cases, is a mouth and an opinion. Most people have an abundance of both. Even though some people are very good at being critics, it really doesn't take much effort. You don't even have to know what you are talking about to be good at it.

You may find this interesting. Since the beginning of time, to the best of my knowledge, the world has never erected a statue to a critic. Think about that for a moment.

A writer once made the observations that

those that can, do, and those that can't, criticize.

Criticism provides a source of instant gratification. How many meetings have you attended where someone would present an idea and almost immediately someone else would point out reasons why that idea won't work? The critic receives quick satisfaction from his or her criticism. The meeting usually then moves on to other matters. The committee members do not have to do anything.

However, when new ideas are presented, there is a significant amount of energy and effort required to turn ideas into reality. But when criticism dominates discussion and thinking, little energy and effort is required.

Theodore Roosevelt said it best in a speech he delivered. Part of his talk has been entitled:

To Dare Greatly

It is not the critic who counts;
not the man
who points out how the strong
man stumbled or where the
could have done th
The credit belon
who is actuall
who
marred by dust
who str
who errs and c
again;

marred by dust and sweat and blood;
who strives valiantly;
who errs and comes short again and
again; who knows
the great enthusiasm,
the great devotions,
and spends himself in a worthy
cause; who at the best,
knows the triumph of high achievement;
and who at the worst,
if he fails,
at least fails
while daring greatly
so that his place shall
never be with those cold and timid souls
who neither knew victory nor defeat.

The arena of life is full of critics. Beware of them! Remember, it is always easier to destroy than it is to build. What do you think?

Little Bitty Minds Can Travel In Large Groups

One of the most serious threats to an individual's unique humanity is the misguided desire to move with the crowd; to do what everyone else is doing; to be like everyone else. This pursuit, this desire to be like everyone else, is a sure way to become average.

Average thinking and performance do not make things happen.

History provides evidence that in too many situations, the crowd tends to be wrong. Too often, we find people justifying their actions by stating that everybody's doing it. If we allow what everybody else is doing to determine what we should be doing, we may find ourselves doing what nobody should be doing.

This crowd-like mentality implies a kind of slave mentality, a form of mass motivation. When people do things because of what others have told them they should be doing, they are relinquishing their individuality, their uniqueness. This doesn't mean that people should not stop at red lights and obey the laws that are necessary for an effectively functioning society. What it does suggest however, is that we need to be more aware of where we are getting our advice from and who our role models are. In many instances, people seem to be following people who don't know anymore than they do.

Average thinking and performance do not make things happen. All progress and growth stem from a desire to rise above averageness.

No one wants to be average. There are no average people, there are just people who think average. Rather than playing follow the leader, we play follow the follower. The justification for performance or lack of performance is the war cry, "everybody's doing it." As a result, we develop a form of crowd morality.

...some have defined conscience as God's presence in man.

This crowd morality, produces a sea of mediocrity and confusion. No matter how many people shirk their responsibilities on the job, shirking responsibilities is wrong. No matter how many people steal, stealing is wrong. No matter how many people take drugs, taking drugs is wrong. No matter how many people commit violence, violence is wrong. No matter how many illegitimate births there are, illegitimate births are wrong.

The fact that any misdeed becomes popular does not make it permissible. As a society, our persistent, quiet acceptance of misdeeds gradually numbs our sense of rightness and morality. By our actions or inactions, we are working to silence the voice of conscience that is in all of us. But, it can't be done. The more we seek to silence that internal voice, the more it cries out to be heard and the more inner emptiness we feel. The actions of the crowd cannot silence the inner voice of conscience. You may find it interesting that some have defined conscience as God's presence in man.

The challenge for each of us is to rise above the temptation to move with the crowd. Each of us must vigilantly work to be true to ourselves, to be true to the best that is in each of us. What do you think?

How Good A Thinker Are You?

"Thinking is the ultimate human resource. Yet we can never be satisfied with our most important skill. No matter how good we become, we should always want to be better." With these words, Dr. Edward de Bono captures some fundamental ideas regarding the skill of thinking. He is regarded as the leading, international authority in teaching thinking as a skill.

Thinking is a skill that is often taken for granted, much like breathing. It is a given, that we can all breath. It is also a given that we can all think. The question becomes, "What is the quality of our breathing and thinking?"

If you wanted to become competitive in any field of athletics, would your normal, everyday breathing skills be sufficient, or would you have to develop improved skills to enhance your endurance and your ability to process oxygen more effectively? Obviously, your everyday breathing skills which get you through the day, would not be sufficient to enable you to have the stamina, strength and endurance to be competitive in serious athletics.

How about your thinking skills? Do you think that your everyday thinking skills are sufficient to get you through the challenges that life keeps throwing your way? Most people don't think much about thinking skill levels. They more or less assume that because they can think, they think well. Does it make sense to also assume that because you can breathe, you breathe well?

Dr. De Bono provides some very powerful insights into the concept of viewing thinking from the perspective of being a skill. He suggests that most peoples' thinking is ego-centered, ego-defensive and focuses on proving themselves right.

He also speculates that most of the difficulties in thinking effectiveness are caused by confusion. People seek to do too many things at the same time when they think. They deal with emotions, logic, creativity information, hope and more. The frequent result is that thinking breaks down and becomes confused and ineffective.

From De Bono's research, most people are complacent about their thinking because they cannot see how they can become better. If a person already sees himself as a good thinker, he is likely to do nothing about becoming a better one.

> *"Wealth is the product of man's capacity to think."*
> *— Ayn Rand*

The first step in becoming a better thinker is intention, wanting to become one. This is both easy and difficult. As with all skill development, it requires practice. But, you will want to know what to practice. You will want to get some new information. You will want to develop some new benefits about what effective thinking is and what it is not. You will want to understand why being right all the time is not good thinking. You will want to understand why being clever is not good thinking. You will, in effect, need to learn how to redefine thinking.

How much do you really know about thinking? How many books have you read about it? How many courses have you taken that actually focused on thinking as a skill? For most people, the answers to these questions would suggest that thinking is just something that is taken for granted. Most people just work throughout their day with the same thinking skills they had last year. They rarely ever question their need to continually sharpen their skills.

If you would like to do some research on thinking skills and work on developing yours, you would find De Bono's book "Six Thinking Hats" an excellent source. In the words of Ayn Rand, "Wealth is the product of man's capacity to think." What do you think?

What You See, Is Not Always What You Get

Beauty in our society is often judged by external appearances rather than internal strengths.

Have you ever been influenced by the "Diner Effect?" What is the "Diner Effect?" Well, it works like this. Can you remember going to a diner late at night? You know, maybe after a movie, or a night out. Many diners have their dessert displays filled with large, sumptuous looking, luscious, appetizing, fattening, attractive looking cakes, pies, puddings, etc. positioned right near their entrance. Some people walking into a diner have been known to gasp for air as they view the tempting array of sinful treats.

You know what happens next. You fall to the temptation. You order one of those breath-taking looking desserts. But, somehow, when it arrives, and you taste it, it doesn't quite measure up to your expectations. It just doesn't match its appearance. There's just something missing. You don't know exactly what it is, but it's just not what you had anticipated.

I call this the "Diner Effect." It happens when we become enchanted by appearances and we allow the appearances to be the principle influence on our judgments and decisions. How often have our decisions and judgments, based primarily on appearances, proven to be poor ones?

In looking at our society, it would appear that we have become very cosmetic in many areas of life. Our society has become so focused on external appearances that it has lost sight of the importance of internal fundamentals. The internal fundamentals, like the internal ingredients of a dessert, make the differences in life.

The internal ingredients of a happy, productive life include values like, trust, honesty, integrity, sincerity, courage, love, persistence, responsibility, and compassion. Beauty in our society is often judged by external appearances rather than internal strengths. External beauty is fleeting. Appearances can easily be deceiving. We know these things, yet how often do we allow ourselves to become victims to the externals rather than working to understand the internals?

It is interesting to note that as a society, we are the wealthiest in the history of the world. But, our wealth is most often measured in externals. The number of cars we own, the size of our homes, the number of TVs, VCRs, stereos we own, the number of vacations we take a year, and many other external criteria. These are too often used as measures of wealth.

If we are the wealthiest society, why do so many people seem so unhappy? Why are

"Things are not always what they seem; the first appearance deceives many; the intelligence of few perceives what has been carefully hidden in the recesses of the mind."
-Phaedrus

there so many divorces? Why is there so much drug and alcohol use? Could it be that too many people are caught up in the "Diner Effect?" Could it be that too many of us have become so preoccupied with appearances that we have lost sight of many of the most important, internal factors that really produce wealth? True wealth and happiness comes from the acquisition of mental, internal fundamentals rather than the external, cosmetic ones.

Beware of the "Diner Effect!" It is very easy to get caught up in appearances. In the words of Phaedrus, "Things are not always what they seem; the first appearance deceives many; the intelligence of few perceives what has been carefully hidden in the recesses of the mind." What do you think?

Let's Hear It For The Dreamers

Thoreau stated, "If one advances confidently in the direction of his dreams, and endeavors to live the life which he had imagined, he will meet with a success unexpected in common hours." As we look around our world today, how many of us could be called dreamers?

Can you remember your early childhood? What were some of your dreams? It seems that when we were young, it was much easier to be a dreamer. Adults didn't tell you not to dream. They were often amused and encouraging as they listened to your hopes and dreams of the future.

Somehow, in the process of becoming an adult, we lose our ability to dream. While adults believe it's perfectly all right and natural for children to dream, adults themselves confess that they don't dream any more, and if they do, they just have nightmares.

Everything you see around you is the result of someone's dream. The car you drive, the TV you watch, the jet you fly in, all of these results from a dream. So why don't we have more dreamers today?

It may be because we have so many dream-stealers around today. A dream-stealer is

"If one advances confidently in the direction of his dreams, and endeavors to live the life which he has imagined, he will meet with a success unexpected in common hours."
-Thoreau

41

anyone who tells you what you are not able to do. In most cases, these are people who have never really accomplished anything themselves and who therefore believe that you won't either, so you shouldn't waste your time dreaming. They are quick to point out the shortcomings of any new idea. They are the people who are most comfortable performing in the role of the devil's advocate. They are the 'but' people. They consistently get their 'buts' in the way of someone's dream. They are forever holding up the wheels of progress.

Beware

of the

dream-stealers!

Beware of the dream-stealers! They are everywhere. You will find them in classrooms and boardrooms. They are in the media and in your neighborhood. They can even be in your family.

Don't let anybody steal your dream! If you have a dream be very careful of where you get your advice. Most people who have accomplished anything meaningful will be the first to encourage you to go for your dream.

Walt Disney, one of the greatest dreamers of all time, constantly had people telling him he was crazy, even his closest friends. He however, had a very interesting philosophy. If he had an idea, and the vast majority of people told him it wouldn't work, he went for it. His dream of making feature length cartoon movies was repeatedly shot down by people who were convinced that no one would sit through a 90 minute cartoon.

His dream became a reality with the first animated cartoon, a little thing entitled "Snow White And the Seven Dwarfs." The rest, as they say, is history. Disney never stopped dreaming. Even in death, his body is frozen with the dream that when a cure for his disease is discovered he will return to life.

You are, no doubt, aware of the dreamers who have impacted your everyday world. Dreamers like Thomas Edison, Ray Kroc of McDonalds, the Wright brothers, Sam Walton of Wal-Mart, Thomas Watson of IBM and Steven Jobs of Apple Computer. But what about a dreamer like Jeff Blatnick?

Blatnick had a dream to win an Olympic gold medal in Greco-Roman wrestling. He did in 1984. However, in order to achieve his dream, he had to overcome cancer twice.

How about the professional soccer player from Madrid who was living his dream until an automobile accident paralyzed him for over a year and a half, and wiped out his dream. A nurse gave him a guitar to pass the time. While he had no musical experience to that point in his life, he was able to develop a new dream. His name was Julio Inglesias.

Dreams
are what fuel
the progress
of mankind.

43

Pete Strudwick was born without arms or legs. He was still able to fulfill one of his dreams. He is a marathon runner who has already run over 25,000 miles. What do you think people told him when he shared his dream?

And then we have 12 year old, Steven Spielberg who wanted to become a movie director. His dream seems to be going well.

Craig MacFarland was blinded at the age of 2. But that didn't stop him from getting 103 gold medals in athletic competition including golf, skiing and wrestling. Just imagine, he is blind and plays golf. I can see, and I still can't play golf.

Dreams are what fuel the progress of mankind. Our country was built by dreamers, something we all too often forget. So why not strengthen your dream building skills? Read about the dreamers of the past. Find out what they had to overcome and how they did it. A dream coupled with action can change the world.

In the words of George Bernard Shaw, "The reasonable man adapts himself to the world; the unreasonable one persists in trying to adapt the world to himself. Therefore, all progress depends on the unreasonable man." Don't let the dream-stealers make you one of their victims. Get your advice from people who have made their dreams come true. Don't let anybody steal your dream!!! What do you think?

Developing The Skill Of Failure

Do you know how to fail? This might seem like a strange question, but think about it. Most people don't know how to fail.

The failure rate in any activity is in direct correlation to your familiarity with that activity. If the activity is fairly routine, and you are familiar with it, there is a high probability for correctness.

How do you define failure?

If on the other hand, you are working in a new area, if you are looking to be original or creative, you are going to make a lot of mistakes, and be wrong a lot.

What rules or beliefs do you carry around in your mind about mistakes and failure? Most of us have developed a rather defensive mentality about failure that suggests that we should not fail in public. As a result, we don't work at failing. Thomas Watson, the man who started IBM, had a very interesting belief about failure. He believed that the way people become successful was by doubling their failure rate.

This leads to a very powerful question. How do you define failure? Too often, people define failure in such a way that it is almost impossible for them to succeed.

Failure is
A State of
Mind.

If they don't achieve what they want, when they want it and exactly the way they want it, they believe they have failed.

On the other hand, the innovators, the people who are creative, define failure in such a way that it is practically impossible for them to fail. They understand that when they venture out into new territory, when they work at developing new ideas or skills, they will be opening the door for more mistakes and failures. But, they don't look at failure like everybody else. They define failure as a condition that happens only when they don't learn something. As long as they have learned something from an experience, they haven't failed. They believe that you can't learn from something you haven't experienced.

This is a very resourceful and empowering way to define failure. With the many challenges life throws your way, your ability to define failure as the absence of learning, positions you to strengthen your "risk muscles" and experiment with new ideas and new approaches. This is true whether you are individual or an organization. A very powerful question that should be continually asked as you move into new areas is, "What can I learn from this experience?" This question focuses the powers of your mind in a positive, resourceful direction. It challenges you to think of the benefits from an experience that, initially, may have seemed a failure. It

Why not accept the belief that there is no failure, there is only feedback.

forces you to look deeper into the experience to come up with something that you can learn from and use as a building block for future growth.

Many people and organizations operate based on sets of rules and regulations that they have developed over time. These rules and regulations, when they were first developed were based on reasons that made sense at that time. But, things change. Unfortunately, those rules stay in place. They go unchallenged. The more rules and regulations you have, the more frustrations and difficulties you will have dealing with the challenges of life and change.

To effectively deal with change and growth, you will want to examine your definition and your rules about failure. Why not accept the belief that there is no failure, there is only feedback. We all have a right to fail, as long as that failure does not severely hurt us or others. When the opportunity to fail is taken away, the opportunity to learn is denied, and with it, the opportunity to grow and to contribute. What do you think?

Life And Nature

It is amazing the insights you can develop about life by just observing Nature. When the Fall season arrives, it provides us an interesting study on life and human growth.

For most people, Fall is a time for observing the beautiful colorings of Nature as it prepares for the challenges of Winter. The Spring and Summer growth of trees and shrubs is brought to an abrupt halt. Plant life recedes inward for protection in anticipation of the environmental factors of Winter. In the colder regions, this process is necessary in order for continued life and growth in the plant world.

If we were to relate this to human life, we would get an interesting analogy. In plant life, growth is in spurts during the Spring and Summer months. This growth is followed by a period of apparent non-growth and dormancy during the Fall and Winter months. Human learning and growth must also go through the same cycles. Meaningful learning whether in the arts, the sciences, music, athletics or anything else, requires periods of what would appear, at least externally, to be non-growth.

Think back in your own life. Have there even been periods when you were learning something and you were working and practicing very hard, and there seemed to be little, if any improvement? Perhaps, you were learning something new and in the beginning of your learning, you made great strides. You were able to see your growth and improved performance. You were probably very excited. But, very often, this growth was followed by a period where nothing seemed to be happening. You weren't seeing any improvement. You were doing all the right things yet you were not getting the improved results you wanted. You were on what might be called a learning plateau.

All learning requires that we experience these plateaus, periods were nothing seems to be happening. This is one of the most frustrating aspects of the learning process. It is much like the dormancy in Nature during the Fall and Winter. Even though it appears externally, that there is no growth, the development is internal. Nature is, internally building the basis for the growth of Spring.

What makes learning and growth so difficult is that we must fight our way through these periods of apparent non-growth. We must fight very hard to overcome the temptation to quit, because it is so easy when we don't see the growth we expected from all our hard work. If you have ever been on a diet, you will be able to identify with this idea. When you start

All learning requires periods of "learning plateaus."

a diet, you are excited because you see the rapid early weight loss. But, after you have been working and sacrificing so hard, you find little or no further loss. This becomes very discouraging and the temptation to quit becomes stronger and stronger. It is at this point that most people give-in and abandon their diet.

By better understanding how the learning and growing process works, you will be better able to accept those flat, plateau times when the results you are looking for are not so obvious. What is actually happening, is that you are developing both the physical and mental foundations necessary for the learning and growth spurts that will come if you just keep on working at it. This same process works in athletics, music, and any other area. Just as with growth plateaus in Nature, plateaus are a necessary part of the human growth process. In fact, it is not uncommon to spend much growing time, in what externally at least, appears non-growth. Too often, growth is occurring so gradually at times, that we are not aware it is happening. If you have ever watched children grow, you will be able to relate with this. Their growth is so gradual that all of a sudden, one day, you realize that they have grown.

So, as you enjoy the beauty of nature this Fall, remember, it's part of Nature's mas-

ter growth plan. As a Chinese proverb
suggests, "Don't be afraid of growing
slowly, be afraid only of standing still."
What do you think?

"Don't be afraid

of growing

slowly, be afraid

of standing still."

— Chinese Proverb

The Wisdom Of The Ages

Suppose someone asked you to summarize all the wisdom of the great philosophers throughout history into one sentence. Could you do it? Just imagine, combining the wisdom of Socrates, Plato, Thomas Acquinas, Confucius, Camus, Lao Tzu, Locke, Descartes, Spinoza (the list can go on and on) into one sentence. What would your sentence be?

"There are no free lunches in life."

How about this one, "There are no free lunches in life."? Do you think this one sentence can do justice to the great thinkers of history? It suggests that everything has a price and that nothing is gotten without some kind of cost or effort.

It communicates a belief that what we do, or what we don't do, at some point in time, will produce a result or outcome. This result or outcome may be very gradual over time. It may be so gradual that we may not realize it is happening until it is too late.

If you think about it long enough, you will find that this one sentence can be applied to anything in life. It can be applied to the way you eat, drink, think, learn, love, exercise, work, etc.

How often do you find people looking for something for nothing? How often do you see and hear people looking for something of value that can be gotten with little or no effort. These people seem to approach life as if it were a lottery. They seem to be looking for opportunities to buy lottery tickets for life, hoping they will get lucky. Their battle cry is, "Hey, you never know!"

This kind of lottery thinking can be very self-destructing not only for individuals but also for societies. Getting something for nothing, in the long-run, does not build strength and power. It builds weakness and dependency.

A few summers ago, I spent a week vacationing in Bar Harbor, Maine. Bar Harbor is an area with a lot of natural beauty. One of the popular things to do, was to take a boat tour that traveled the waterways around Bar Harbor. Passengers were able to see whales, seals, and other water-life close up and personal. Part of the excitement of this tour was the chance to catch a glimpse of a bald eagle. Bald eagles are an endangered species and at that time, a pair of them had mated on one of the small uninhabited islands that surround Bar Harbor. They had given birth to a pair of eaglets, so the chances of seeing an eagle were greatly increased. Passengers roamed the decks of these tour boats with excited anticipation, armed with cameras and binoculars.

One of the boat captains had thought of a clever way to guarantee that his passengers would see the eagles. As he approached their island, he would throw food into the water and then toot the boat's horn. Over time, the young eaglets became conditioned to expect food when they heard the sound of the boat's horn. So, whenever they heard the toot of the horn they flew out to be fed. They were apparently getting a free lunch, without having to invest the time and effort to hunt. The passengers on the boat were happy, they saw the eagles and the eagles were happy because they were getting fed. It seemed like a win/win situation. However, remember our no free lunches in life philosophy. There are long-run implications from apparent short-run free lunches.

It wasn't long before people began to realize that these boats did not conduct tours during the late Fall and Winter months. This meant that if the young eaglets became too accustomed to being fed, they would not develop their hunting skills sufficiently to survive during the Fall and Winter months. As a result, a resolution was passed forbidding anyone to feed the eagles.

The same kind of reasoning can be applied to humans. Each of us should give some serious thought to the long-term implications that can result from apparent free lunches, both for ourselves and for others. The perception of getting something for nothing needs to be challenged. Too often, by focusing on short-term benefits, we can easily lose sight of the creation of long-term problems. What do you think?

Holiday Gifts
For Kids

If you have ever walked through a toy store at holiday time, it can be a very challenging and humbling experience. It seems that every year, there are always certain toys that are hot, and almost every child has them on their gift list. In 1995, the hot items were Power Ranger toys. They generated about $300 million in retail sales. Imagine, $300 million.

The more high-tech our world becomes, the more it seems to reduce the need for individual thinking, imagination and creativity.

It is always very interesting to watch children at play, especially in today's world. If you look at the array of toys children have, it can easily boggle the mind. In our modern age of technology, there are toys that talk to you, record your own voice, make all kinds of noises and sound effects, fly, self-destruct, and the list goes on and on. In the high-tech area, we have the big ticket items like Nintendo and Sega Genesis.

An interesting question to ask is, "Why do people buy certain toys for children?" How many toys stimulate a child's mind and imaginatiion? How many toys help children to think and to learn?

Take Power Ranger toys for example. These toys result from the #1 rated children TV show in 1995, the Mighty Morphin Power Rangers. This show in-

*What did you
enjoy playing
with most, when
you were a child?*

volved a group of teenagers who transformed themselves into powerful warriors who fought evil. It created such a phenomena that children, all across the country, from the age of three and up, could at any time, erupt into wild, Bruce Lee type behavior. You could actually see, small children kicking and karate-chopping their way through their schools and their neighborhoods. Is this the kind of behavior we want to encourage in our children? How do children benefit from their Power Ranger experience? Isn't this a classic example of how the media, in this case TV, can create and impact a child's behavior?

The more high-tech our world becomes, the more it seems to reduce the need for individual thinking, imagination and creativity. How many toys encourage the use of imagination? When children watch TV and videos, they are dazzled and mesmerized by sophisticated graphic special effects and Dolby sound. There seems to be very little left to the imagination. How many children read books these days? Reading is one of the most powerful ways to stimulate imagination because you have to provide your own mental special effects and sounds. Do you think it's possible that one of the reasons children may become bored so easily, even though they have all these sophisticated toys, is because they are not challenged to use their mind and their imagination?

What did you enjoy playing with most when you were a child? Was it something that required you to use your mind, your imagination and your creativity?

Have you ever watched children play with, of all things, a large empty box? Maybe it was for a TV or something larger. It is amazing how long something like that can keep their interest.

One Christmas, Santa (me) brought my children a giant Tinker Toy set. It had some pieces that were 3 feet long. They enjoyed that set for years. They used blankets and whatever else they could think of to enhance their constructed figures. The only thing that limited their use of this toy was their imagination.

"Imagination is more important than knowledge."
-Albert Einstein

Remember, in our desire to make a child happy, giving them what they want, may not be in the best interest of the child. We, as adults, have the power and the ability to think on a longer-term basis. Children do not, they think for the moment.

A child's mind and imagination are precious and fragile. They need to be stimulated and nurtured in positive ways. If a child's mind and imagination are not stimulated positively in youth, their use, in later life, may be restricted.

One of the keys to success and happiness in life is having a strong, active imagina-

tion. Many of the challenges of life
require imaginative and creative solu-
tions. In the words of Albert Einstein,
"Imagination is more important then
knowledge." What do you think?

New Year Resolutions

With the arrival of each new year, if you are like most people, you decide to begin it with good intentions for positive change and personal growth.

You tell yourself that THIS will be the year you really commit to your New Year's resolutions. This year, you will really discipline yourself to do those one or two things you have wanted to do for a long time. How many times have you told yourself this? And, how many times, even with the best intentions, have you failed to keep your commitment to yourself? Here are some ideas that may help to keep you on that road to achievement.

To help strengthen your commitment to what you want to accomplish, you will want to understand some key ideas related to the goal setting process. Just having a goal is not enough.

Idea #1: Don't think in terms of a goal or goals. Think rather in terms of an outcome or a result. If you are like most people, you have used the term goal many times and have not achieved what you wanted. As a result, the term goal has not been one that is too empowering for you. Replace it with the term OUTCOME or RESULT. You will not always be successful in

Don't think

in terms

of a

goal or goals.

achieving your goals, but you will always be successful in achieving results. So, think in terms of the results or outcomes you desire to produce.

Idea #2: It is important to WRITE down specifically what result or outcome you want to accomplish. Writing is a form of thought discipline. By writing something down, you force yourself to think. And, since you are writing, you force yourself to think more clearly than if you just allow your thoughts to float around in your head. Writing also enables you to SEE your thoughts. This process of seeing is very powerful because most of us are visual learners and by seeing, specifically what we are thinking, helps us to be more focused in our understanding.

Idea #3: Write down WHY you want to produce this outcome or result. This will be one of your most powerful resources in your understanding the process of achievement. WHY you want to achieve something is key to your commitment and energy levels. It is the driving force behind your efforts. It is often the single reason most people do not sustain their initial effort in achieving their results. They don't have a strong enough WHY. When you have a strong enough WHY, your mind will become more creative in developing the techniques or the HOWs of accomplishment.

Write, Write, Write.

Idea #4: WRITE down the benefits/rewards you will receive from achieving your desired outcome. The more benefits you can write down, the greater will be your desire to overcome the challenges you will face on the way to achieving your desired results. Again, the key work here is WRITE.

Idea #5: WRITE down the key obstacles you anticipate could prevent you from achieving your desired results. This may seem like a strange idea, but once again, by writing things down, you crystallize your thinking. As long as obstacles exist in your mind, they can seem insurmountable. Your mind can be a very dark and dangerous place to live. Somehow, psychologically, by seeing things on paper, they will not appear as menacing as if they just existed in your mind.

Idea #6: Set a written deadline. Put some kind of time horizon on your expected outcome. Without a written deadline, you will not have a sense of urgency. There will always be tomorrow. You can always tell yourself that you will start tomorrow. With a written date for accomplishment, psychologically, you will keep the pressure on yourself. As you can see, writing is a very powerful tool in accomplishing improved results. By strengthening your ability to write your ideas down, you are strengthening the power of your thinking. And, as you strengthen your powers of

thought, you will strengthen your powers of accomplishment. What do you
think!

And The Pursuit of Happiness

Happiness has been described as one of life's most elusive victories. In today's rapidly changing, high tech society, happiness seems increasingly more difficult to attain because we see so many false images of it.

The philosopher Immanuel Kant argued that man should not seek to be happy but "to be deserving of happiness." He believed that happiness was something that had to be earned rather than pursued.

Man is born to struggle.

As we look around society today, there is a growing belief that happiness is a 'right' and that society's mission is to provide happiness for everyone. This belief, if it continues to spread, will serve to produce the opposite effect...unhappiness, frustration and pain.

I would like to suggest that happiness comes when we are in pursuit of an important objective; when we are in the process of achieving something meaningful.

In this pursuit, as in any meaningful pursuit, there will be struggle. It is the struggle that makes victory worthwhile. Without the struggle, victory loses much of its meaning.

65

We live in

an age of

instant mashed

potatoes.

Man is born to struggle. It is through 'the struggle', that we build ourselves and our 'children'. Today, there seems to be a growing desire to avoid many of the struggles and adversities of life. Too many people are looking for someone or something, be it the government or the family or the organization, to remove the obstacles that produce the struggles in life. But, without obstacles, can there be any real meaningful victory and growth? It is only through our working to overcome the many obstacles in life that we become strong, both mentally and physically.

We live in an age of instant mashed potatoes. We have developed a "quick-fix" mentality that wants things NOW. We have somehow lost an understanding for the importance of the principle of delayed gratification. It has become very easy to confuse pleasure with happiness.

Pleasure, with its "quick-fix", feel good nature, is a short-term, easily attained objective. Happiness, on the other hand, is a more difficult to attain, long-term one. Happiness can be described as a state of being and not an end result.

It is the nature of man to never be satisfied, to always be stretching. We usually do not seek things for their own sake, but for the thrill of the quest. It is the overcoming of obstacles that make the chase worthwhile. But, if we seek to avoid the obstacles, if we seek to have others remove those obstacles, can that "state of being" called happiness ever be ours?

Our nation was built by people who continually worked to overcome obstacles. They understood the importance of the principle of "delayed gratification". They understood that no matter what obstacle they had, if they kept their feet on the ground and kept moving in the right direction, they would someday arrive at their destination. Their character was built and strengthened by this belief.

"Our prayers are answered, not when we are given what we ask, but when we are challenged to be what we can be."
-Morris Adler

Whether we are parents raising children, educators developing young minds or managers developing employees, we should continually work to instill an understanding for the need for adversity in the growth process. Accepting adversity and the principle of "delayed gratification" will position us for greater growth and happiness in the 21st century. In the words of Morris Adler, "Our prayers are answered, not when we are given what we ask, but when we are challenged to be what we can be." What do you think?

Hard And Soft Learning

What prevents people from learning as they go through life? There are many possible reasons. Recently, while experiencing some frustration during a management development program I was conducting, I began to give some serious thought to this question.

I was working with a group of professionals who had been successful in moving up the so called "ladder of success," but somehow, they were in a valley that was preventing them from moving both themselves and their organization forward effectively.

This is common situation. Many organizations experience the same thing. People, for some unexplained reason, seem to stop learning. What contributes to this condition?

After some considerable thought, it occurred to me that when most people get their first "real" job, they usually are hired because they have certain "hard" skills. They have knowledge of engineering, finance, nursing, computers, medicine or some other area. They have developed some hard knowledge that can be of benefit to an organization.

What prevents people from learning as they go through life?

69

As they achieve success within their organization and begin to advance through the ranks, their hard knowledge and skill, while still important, becomes less important. A need for greater "soft" skills in such areas as interpersonal relations, communication, and "problem" solving arises.

The difficulty is that people have become very skilled at developing "hard" knowledge because, for the most part, they can develop this on their own. They can go to school, read books and trade magazines and go to seminars and continue to build this hard knowledge base.

Soft skills, on the other hand, cannot be learned alone. They are not a product of a single individual's efforts, but require the collaborative efforts of others. They require interaction, trust, public mistakes and failures. In short, soft skills mandate "public practice." This willingness to "practice in public" on an ongoing basis is at the foundation for effective "teamwork" whether at home, at the office, at school, or in everyday living. It is teamwork that is at the heart of organizational and societal growth and development.

The development of "soft" skills demands that individuals incur risk; a risk that may open them to criticism from others. This risk also requires they share a part of themselves with others. It is through this acceptance of risk that we grow as individuals, organizations and a society.

The following words best capture the essence of this risk:

To Risk

To laugh is to risk appearing the fool.
To weep is to risk appearing sentimental.
To reach out for another is to risk involvement. To expose feelings is to risk exposing our true self.
To place your ideas, your dreams before the crowd is to risk loss.
To love is to risk not being loved in return.
To live is to risk dying.
To hope is to risk despair.
To try at all is to risk failure.
But to risk we must, because the greatest hazard in life is to risk nothing.
The man, the woman, who risks nothing, does nothing, has nothing, is nothing.
-Anonymous

What do you think?

It is teamwork that is at the heart of organizational and societal growth and development.

Beware Of the Invisible Horses

It happened in England during World War II. British Intelligence had uncovered a plot by the Nazis to invade England by way of the English Channel.

To combat this attack, men who were not actively involved in the war effort were assembled on the cliffs of Dover where they were trained to fire artillery weapons at moving targets in the channel.

We are holding our own invisible horses.

After months of training, these artillery crews were filmed in action. This film was then sent to the War Department in London, where military leaders were to evaluate their progress.

As they watched the film, these military experts noticed that a few of the gunnery crew-men exhibited a rather strange, unexplainable behavior. Just before the artillery guns were fired, a handful of them stood rigidly still for five to ten seconds.

When the film was over, the evaluators began to discuss the possible motivation for such unusual behavior. After a period of unproductive discussion, they decided to watch the film again.

73

During this second viewing, a general entered the room to observe the film. Again, when the film was over, another discussion was begun in an effort to uncover the possible reasons for the men's unusual behavior. It was during this discussion that the newly arrived general stood up and stated that it was obvious to him, that these men were holding the horses. This comment was received with laughter by the other officers in the room because there were no horses in the film.

The general was very serious. He went on to point out that since most of England's younger men were already active in the war effort, these men were much older and he suggested that many of them had served during World War I. He reminded the other officers that during World War I, artillery pieces were transported on caissons drawn by horses. Certain men had the responsibility of keeping the horses steady before the guns were fired. The general speculated that the men who were exhibiting this strange behavior must have had that responsibility. He concluded that they were in effect holding invisible horses. They were carrying a habit, which they had developed 25 years ago, and bringing it forward into the future, even though it was no longer effective.

Most of us do the same thing. We are holding our own invisible horses. These are habits of thinking and behaving that were effective for us in the past, but are no longer effective in today's world. And, like those men, we are not aware we are doing it.

You can see this invisible horse effect throughout our society. You can see it in organizations, in politics, in education and in the personal lives of people everyday.

Fortunately, there are certain key signs that can alert you to the presence of these invisible horses. You will find them present when you hear phrases like: "We have always done it this way," "That's just the way I am, I'll never change," "You can't teach an old dog new tricks," "That won't work, we tried it once," "That's just the way we do things around here," "Sorry, that's our policy," and the list can continue.

The bottom line is that you will want to become more aware of the existence of some of your own invisible horses. By becoming aware of their existence, you will be able to challenge them, and at the same time work to eliminate those that are holding you back from what you want to accomplish. By asking questions like; "What if...?", "Is there a better way to do this?" "What would I have to do to make this work?" "How can we do this and have fun at the same time?" "Where am I getting my new ideas from?" you will be able to challenge those limiting invisible horses. What do you think?

If...

"If you can keep your head when all about you are losing theirs and blaming it on you..." is the opening line of Rudyard Kipling's poem, IF. As you look around society, do you ever think that we may be losing our collective head? To help answer this question, you may want to consider some of the following events.

A jury, recently awarded a woman $2.9 million in damages as a result of burns she received after spilling a cup of McDonald's coffee on herself. The fact that she had placed the coffee between her legs and was traveling in the car at the time didn't seem to enter into the jury's decision.

It was reported in Massachusetts that a young man stole a car from a shopping center parking lot and was killed while driving it. The owner of the parking lot was then sued by the boy's family on the grounds that the owner had not taken sufficient precautions to prevent such thefts.

How about the man with a 60 inch waist? He threatened to sue a fast food restaurant chain because he felt his civil rights were being violated. Since he couldn't fit into the seats in the restaurant, and since he was part of a minority group (the large and

CAUTION:

Engage Your Brain

Before Using

This Product...

Common Sense

is Not Very

Common.

heavy minority), he felt the restaurant chain was discriminating against him.

And then we have the case of an employee who was fired for continually showing up late for work. The employee then sued his former employer because he claimed that he suffers from what his lawyer called "chronic lateness disorder."

It seems that everywhere you look these days, somebody or some group is claiming that they are victim of something, something that they have no control over. If you spill hot coffee between your legs, and burn yourself, it is apparently not your fault that you made a decision to carry it there and then travel in a moving car. You are a victim of some organization that makes its coffee too hot. Maybe McDonalds should print a disclaimer on all its hot liquids cautioning customers to avoid contact with human skin. Or, maybe organizations should label all products with the following label, "The use of this product without the appropriate use of COMMON SENSE may be hazardous to either your physical or mental health, or both." Or, perhaps a universal disclaimer such as; "Caution: Engage Your Brain Before Using This Product," may be helpful.

Is it possible that stupidity is becoming a disease? Is it possible that people who act without responsibility without common sense, without thinking, and without discipline are becoming labeled as dysfunctional? Is it possible that we, as a society are becoming too casual in our use of the term dysfunctional?

Some have gone as far as to suggest that dysfunction maybe the growth industry of the 21st century.

A society that does not excerise the powers of its collective mind, is sure to lose it.

How can we expect to be productive and happy in a society when we are apparently abandoning our responsibility to use common sense and to hold people responsible for their actions, especially those that appear to be rather stupid ones? Are we fostering the development of a culture of learned helplessness? I certainly hope not. It is up to each of us to see to it we don't get ourselves and others caught up in this wave of helplessness or what some have labeled 'victimism.' The mind is our most powerful resource. A society that does not exercise the powers of its collective mind, is sure to lose it.

So beware of where you put your hot coffee! And remember, common sense is not very common. What do you think?

Progressive Inertia

There is a story told of a 5 year old boy who was visiting his grandfather during the Christmas holidays. This was a very exciting time for the boy because his grandfather lived in a cabin in the snow-covered, back woods of Maine.

One night, while the boy was sitting by the fire, he noticed that his grandfather's old dog, Rusty, was lying snuggled in his favorite spot close to the fire. Every once and a while the old dog would move and would let out a soft moan. After hearing a number of these moans, the boy's curiosity was aroused and he asked his grandfather why the dog moaned. The old man explained that that was Rusty's favorite place to sleep and there is a small nail in the floor board there and every once and a while, when he moves a certain way, he hits that board and he moans because of the pain. "Well, why doesn't he move to another place?" the boy asked. "I guess the pain doesn't bother him that much," the old man replied.

How many people seem to go through life accepting pain because they perceive that the "pain" and "discomfort"of

Change is ongoing and continuous.

81

CHANGE will be greater than the pain they are experiencing in their current circumstances. Change is ongoing and continuous. It is the nature of life. While you are reading this, millions of your cells are dying, and millions are being created. And, there is nothing you can do about it. You are a little older then you were when you started reading this and there is nothing you can do about that either.

There is nothing you can do to stop change. It is life. Today, we are experiencing accelerated rates of change that are unparalleled in the history of the world. Whether, in Health Care, Computers, Banking, Education, Electronics, we are beset by rapid changes.

The question becomes, "How do we effectively handle this change?" Most people respond like that old dog, by doing the same thing and living with the same old "pain" and "discomfort." However, this strategy can lead to a state of PROGRESSIVE INERTIA. For most people, CHANGE represents a threat. It fosters a "fear of the unknown." It suggests a new course of thinking and or action that is perceived as psychologically uncomfortable. As with old Rusty, it just seems easier to stay in that same old "comfortable" spot and endure the pain then it does to move to another spot. For many people, the risk of discomfort

For most people,

CHANGE

represents a threat.

caused by that nemesis, "the fear of the unknown," locks them into inaction.

Upon closer examination, change is actually another term for "growth." It is synonymous with "learning." Without change there can be no real learning? Why do so may people continually think and perform the same way in the presence of change, even though they are experiencing great discomfort? In many instances, it is some form of fear. This fear paralyzes them into a state of "progressive inertia." It could be a fear of failure, of rejection, of criticism, of the unknown or something else.

We all have fears. They are a product of human nature. But many of our fears are more a product of our imagination and creativity than our logic. One way to handle them, since we will never be able to eliminate them, is to use the same powers that created them, to overcome them.

Through our powers of imagination and creativity we can work through our discomfort and pain to focus on the results and benefits we want. By developing a plan and by taking positive action, we can move out of the "inertia" trap of inaction and self-doubt.

It may be a fear of going back to school, or a fear that you are too old to start a

But many of our fears are more a product of our imagination and creativity than our logic.

new career or new job. Whatever it is, the starting point is to take some positive action, to create movement and overcome "inertia." Otherwise, we will be like that old dog that becomes too comfortable and just accepts his pain. Remember, an old dog CAN learn new tricks. What do you think?

An old dog

can learn

new tricks.

The Small Brown Package

The year was 1911. In an impoverished European village, a 9 year old boy sat vigilantly at the bedside of his beloved, ailing grandmother. Sadly, as he thought of the possibility of her death, an old woman entered the room. She stood silently at the foot of the bed for a few moments. Slowly moving to the head of the bed, she placed a small brown package under the grandmother's pillow and left.

The boy did not understand this strange behavior. He immediately opened the package and to his surprise, found two onions. He was very confused. He could not understand why the old woman would do such a thing.

Several weeks later, the young boy met the old woman again. He asked her to explain the significance of the package of onions. The old woman explained that last year, her family was without food and that the boy's grandmother had given them some potatoes. Since his grandmother was so ill, the old woman wanted her to know that her act of kindness was greatly appreciated, so she did the best she could to show her appreciation and gave her the onions.

How often, in our busy, hectic, everyday lives do we take things for granted?

It was from this experience, that a nine year old boy taught himself a most powerful lesson; the lesson of appreciation.

How often, in our busy, hectic, everyday lives do we take things for granted? It is so easy to do. I find myself doing it more than I care to consider. It is so easy to become numb to the kindness and generosities of others. Everyday presents us with opportunities to show someone, whether they are loved ones, friends or even strangers, that we appreciate the little acts of kindness that are directed our way.

The way we communicate our appreciation doesn't have to be anything big or grandiose. It could be as simple as a polite expression like "Thank You" or "Please" or "You're Welcome". These are common courtesies that somehow have been lost in our hurry, hurry society.

A small, brown package of two onions was worth its weight in gold because of what it represented. If we were to look around at all the little things we take for granted, it might cause us to become a little more aware of opportunities to show some appreciation to the many people we deal with everyday. The people in our family, the people who are out there everyday just doing their jobs the best they can.

How about those public servants like the sanitation team that picks up the garbage or the toll collectors who are there day after day handling the many challenges of dealing with the public? How about those people who open your neighborhood deli every morning so you can get your newspaper and coffee or the people in the bagel shop that are there 24 hours a day to satisfy your desires? How about the girl at McDonald's who always seems to have a smile when you go there, or the maintenance crew at the office that does such a good job? How about the receptionist at the office? Those people who work the switchboard, when was the last time you showed them a little appreciation? Or, how about that bus driver who always seems to have a smile on his face or the mail person who always takes care of your mail? What would happen if you sent them a little note just saying thanks? What if you gave them a lottery ticket thanking them for their good work or pleasant smile? What if you brought in a box of donuts or a bag of bagels just to let some group know that you appreciate their hard work? Be creative! I don't think two onions would work but you could give them a shot.

The list can go on and on. The symbolism of the little brown package of onions is a powerful one. By becoming more aware of the many opportunities to show our appreciation for the kindness of others, we feel good and most importantly, they will feel appreciated. What do you think?

The Keeper Of
The Pins

A few years ago, Dionne Warwick had a hit record entitled, "I'll Never Fall In Love Again." Part of the lyric of that song is, "What do you get when you fall in love? You get a lot of pins to burst your bubbles." While the lyric itself refers to love, the concept behind the lyric can be applied to everyday life.

There are a lot of people traveling through life allowing events and other people to be the "pins" that burst their bubbles. How frequently do you hear someone accuse others of making them feel angry, annoyed or upset? How often have you observed people getting upset over little insignificant things that happen during the day? People, for example, who get upset because they were cut off on the highway; or, perhaps because the waitress forgot to bring ketchup for their french fries. Does this make sense? How many times have you witnessed grown, seemingly mature adults, develop "lunatic" behavioral patterns over some silly, unimportant, accidental, dippy, little things?

Think about this a moment. These people are, in effect, allowing other people, in many instances strangers, to be the "keeper of their pins." They are giving these "strangers" control over them. They are allowing the actions

How frequently

do you hear

someone accuse

others of making

them feel angry,

annoyed or upset?

89

of others to control their own reactions, and thus their lives. Does this make sense? We all have bad days. Some people, however, seem to be always having a bad day. These people do not realize that the more they allow the actions of others to affect them, the less control they have over themselves and their lives. The less control a person feels they have over themselves, the more frustrated and negatively stressed they can become.

There is a high correlation between the degree a person feels in control of his or her life and their degree of happiness. People who feel that they are just victims of circumstances have given the control of the "pins" to others. They have given up their power of self-control and as a result, leave a trail of "bubble bursts" in their travels. This belief of "being a victim," can produce much unhappiness and frustration.

People who are the "keepers of their own pins," realize that they ultimately have the power "to choose their responses" to whatever happens to them in life. They realize that in many instances, they have little control over everyday events. They are not able to control whether someone cuts them off on the highway or whether the waitress forgets to bring the ketchup. They have developed the belief that they do have control over their "reaction" to what happens to them. In other words, THEY are the "keepers of their own pins." If their bubble is going to burst, they are the ones who will use the "pins." They do not allow someone else or some event to be in control of those "pins." They work at controlling their own reaction to the actions of others and to outside events.

So, the next time you are feeling down, or angry, or depressed, why not ask yourself, "Who are you allowing to control your pins?"

In the words of a wise old sage, "We are not able to control the wind, but we can adjust the sails." What do you think?

" We are not able to control the wind, but we can adjust the sails."

Do You Have Too Much Old Knowledge?

This might seem like a very strange question, especially if you remember the old adage that, "knowledge is power."

Research suggests that the amount of knowledge in the world is doubling every four to five years. This is mind boggling. The amount of knowledge that exists today, is twice the amount that existed in 1989. By 1999, there will be twice as much as today. We are in a kind of "knowledge revolution." We are being overwhelmed, not only with the amount of knowledge, but with the accelerating rate of its growth. How can we effectively manage this knowledge overload?

The pursuit of knowledge for its own sake, while a worthy endeavor, can prove counterproductive in our modern world. What becomes most important is our focus. Unless you plan to be a game show participant on Jeopardy or a professional Trivial Pursuit competitor, stuffing your brain with just knowledge and information for its own sake, will not be a very rewarding profession. In today's world, "the positive use of knowledge" is a much more meaningful adage than that of "knowledge is power."

Learning today, involves a much clearer fo-

We are in a

kind of

"knowledge revolution."

93

cus on what kind of knowledge we need, where to find it and how to use it. We are living in the age of the "specialist." The age of the generalist is long gone. We find a lot of people have a lot of knowledge and information, but it is old, and it is not up-to-date.

People in recent years have lost jobs, not because they were poor workers, but rather because their knowledge and skills became obsolete for the needs of modern society. They had relied on "old" knowledge about an "old" world, a world that no longer exists. They have too much knowledge, but it's the knowledge of the past. Knowledge that was meaningful ten years ago, but has lost its value in today's world.

Whole industries have experienced this same scenario. Do you remember vinyl records? You know, those old 33 1/3 long playing albums you have somewhere in your house. A few years ago, this was a "billion" dollar industry. People had a lot of knowledge about vinyl records and they had been very successful in that field. But today, we live in a world of "compact discs" and "digital tapes."

If the people who were successful in the vinyl record business wanted to continue their success, they would have had to "dump" their old knowledge of vinyl records and acquire "new" knowledge about CDs and digital recordings.

The positive use of knowledge is power.

And the same can be said of people who cling to knowledge that may have been useful in the past, but today, will only help you on Jeopardy.

The only knowledge that endures over time, is the knowledge that is based on values and principles. The values of honesty, integrity, trust, self-discipline, fairness, respect, are but a few. These values need to be practiced and not just known.

To be competitive in today's rapidly changing environment, our knowledge must be acted upon and continually updated. In the words of Eric Hoffer, "In a time of drastic change, it is the learners who will inherit the world. The learned find themselves living in a world that no longer exists." What do you think?

Are You
A Good
Communicator?

Most people tend to over value their effectiveness as a communicator. Breakdowns in communication are often blamed on the receiver of the message rather than the sender.

What do you think is the most important skill of a good communicator? The answer is listening. Unfortunately, most of us are not good listeners.

Most of us have two ears, two eyes and one mouth. This provides us with basically four input devices and one output device. There is a very good reason for this. We need to be able to listen, not only with our ears, but also with our eyes. Good communicators invest four times as much of their energy and time listening and observing as they do talking. Good communicators need information. They realize that when they are talking, they are not getting information. They are not learning.

What does all this mean? It means that one of the ways to become a better communicator is to invest 80% of your time listening with both your ears and your eyes, and invest only 20% of your time talking. Many people operate in reverse. They spend 80% of their time talking and only 20% of their time listening.

" Seek first to understand, then to be understood,"
is the fifth of
Dr. Stephen Covey's
7 Habits of Highly
Effective People.

Listening is one of the most undeveloped skills in our society.

"Seek first to understand, then to be understood," is the fifth of Dr. Stephen Covey's 7 Habits of Highly Effective People. It is perhaps one of the most difficult of his 7 habits because it demands great discipline and greatly improved skills for most of us. So often, it requires silence, when the need to speak is so strong. So often, it demands that we minimize the importance of the words we are hearing and focus more on the non-verbal messages that are packaging the words. It is these non-verbal messages, the facial expressions, the body movements, the tonality of the words, the breathing patterns of the communicator that are so often at the heart of the message. Too often, we tend to focus more on the words than what is behind the words.

Listening is one of the most undeveloped skills in our society. It is not taught in schools. People don't read books about it. There are few, if any, seminars that effectively provide techniques to improve it.

It is perhaps listening, or more specifically the inability to listen, that accounts for more difficulties, more pain and more suffering in life than just about anything else.

We, as a nation, seem too busy to listen. Good listening is hard work. It doesn't come easy. Most people listen not with the intent to understand, but rather with the intent to reply.

Of all the people that you know, how many would you classify as good listeners? What makes them good listeners? For one thing, they probably do not talk too much. Theyprobably don't judge and evaluate what you say much either. And, they probably don't readily offer you advise unless they believe you are sincerely asking for it.

You can improve the quality of your life by improving the quality of your communication. And, you can improve the quality of your communication by investing time and effort in improving the quality of your listening. Why not become more aware of how often you are listening with just your ears and not your eyes? Why not become more aware of how often you do the talking rather than the listening? Why not become more aware of how often you are really seeking to understand a situation from the other person's perspective before you begin to communicate your own perceptions on the matter?

In the words of John Mapes, "Communication may be the most overworked word and the most underworked act." What do you think?

"Communication may be the most overworked word and the most underworked act."
— John Mapes

Vince Lombardi: A Man For All Seasons

No matter what your job, to achieve success you must be willing to pay a price.

It was a hot, August day in 1959 and he was having one of the worst football practice sessions he had ever experienced. He couldn't do anything right in the eyes of his new coach. He was a professional, yet his coach called him a "cow" and the worst guard he had ever seen. His coach was so disgusted by his performance that he ordered him off the practice field and sent him to the showers.

After practice, when all the players had showered and left, the coach took his usual walk through the locker room. There, still sitting in his uniform, was the 6' 5', 270 pound guard, with his head in his hands, crying. The coach sat beside him and put his arm around his shoulder. He said, "Son, what I said to you today was true. You were doggin' it. But I want you to know, that inside of you is a great football player and I want to help you find him."

That guard was Jerry Kramer of the Green Bay Packers and in 1970, he was named the most outstanding guard in the first 50 years of the NFL. His coach was the legendary Vince Lombardi. And this story illustrates why Vince Lombardi will always be remembered as one of the greatest coaches of all time.

101

Lombardi believed that life required a person's personal commitment to excellence. No matter what your job, to achieve success you must be willing to pay a price. Anything worthwhile demands a price. It demands some sacrifice.

For Lombardi, success was a habit, so was failure. When he took over the Packers in 1959, they had the habit of losing. Their last winning season had been in 1947 when they were 6-5. His first objective was to break them of their losing habits. In particular, he had to change their expectations. Even though they were professionals, prior to 1959, they expected to lose, and they did.

Lombardi's philosophy extended beyond football. It focused on success in life. And, while he was tough on his players, his toughness developed in them the discipline and a mental toughness that enabled them to be successful not only in football, but also in other areas of their lives. Lombardi worked to develop the whole person. He taught his players how to set goals and at the same time, helped them determine the price they were willing to pay to achieve them.

He has often been mis-quoted as saying that "winning is the only thing." In actuality, he stated that,"winning is not everything-but making the effort to win is." He believed that everyone cannot be a winner all the time, but that everyone can make his best effort to win. To Lombardi, the greatest sin was not being true to the best that is in each of us.

Lombardi believed that fatigue made cowards of us all and that most people allow the small hurts in life to get them down everyday. To achieve excellence, you had to learn to play the game of football and the game of life with those small hurts. This, to Lombardi, enabled individuals to develop the mental toughness necessary for any kind of success.

Winning the first time is a lot easier than winning the second time.

The three things in order of importance to Lombardi were: God, family and the Green Bay Packers. He was also a great believer in America. He believed that America's strength came from the desire of its people to win, to be number one. He also felt that there seemed to be a growing sympathy within society only for the losers. This he believed was not right. Lombardi believed that we needed to salute the doers-those who are in the pits day after day making things happen. Progress is achieved by developing the will to win and the will to excel. For the loser, there must be a complete dedication to win the next time. These, to Lombardi, were the qualities that endure. He preached that the quality of an individual's life is a function of their personal commitment to victory and excellence, regardless of their chosen profession.

He disciplined

himself to play

through the

small hurts that

life threw his way.

Winning the first time is a lot easier than winning the second time. How many times have we witnessed a team win a championship, only to lose that championship the next year? How many times have we witnessed a company achieve great success only to lose that success one or two years later? There is a price to pay to stay on top. To repeat as champions, in anything, requires dedication, persistence, self-discipline, and mental toughness. By instilling these qualities in his players, Lombardi was able to take his Packers from being the worst team in professional football to the best. His Packers won three successive NFL Championships and the first two Super Bowls.

The principles and beliefs that produced success for Vince Lombardi and his players were based on Lombardi's belief that he personally needed to continually challenge himself to be the best he could be. He disciplined himself to play through the small hurts that life threw his way. In so doing, he challenged his people to excel and move beyond their own self-limiting beliefs. He became their role model for excellence.

Isn't this one of the things we all want in our lives? Aren't we looking, at times, for some one who believes in us more than we believe in ourselves; some one who will challenge us to reach beyond ourselves and to excel? This is what Vince Lombardi was all about, and this is why he will be remembered as one of the greatest coaches of all time. What do you think?

Look and Pay Attention!

Our brains

operate in

strange ways

at times.

On a recent visit to my favorite bagel store, at 5:30 in the morning, I was intrigued by a sign that was posted by the self-service coffee machines. The sign began with the following words, printed in large block letters: LOOK AND PAY ATTENTION! This introduction was then followed by a series of rules related to using the coffee machines. As I stood reading these rules, which made excellent sense, someone walked up, violated most of the rules, and poured himself a container of coffee.

What most fascinated me, was the heading; LOOK AND PAY ATTENTION! Now, it was 5:30 in the morning, and at that hour it is pretty difficult to do two things at the same time but I began to wonder how often we LOOK but don't pay attention.

I was reminded about the time my couch was stolen. In the past, I have usually only used my garage for storage. Since we were expected to have such an exciting winter, I decided to clean up the garage so I could use it for the car. In addition to my storage habit, I also had the habit of not keeping the garage door locked.

To my surprise, when I went to start the cleanup process, the first thing I noticed was that the couch I had been storing there was gone. I couldn't believe it! Somebody went into the garage and had stolen my couch. Incredible!

I immediately went to tell my wife. She proceeded to inform me that the couch wasn't stolen. I had simply stored it vertically in the corner of the garage to conserve space.

When I went back to the garage, there it was standing up vertically in the left hand corner of the garage, and I hadn't noticed it.

Now, this was a couch! It wasn't a small salt shaker that couldn't be found starring back at you from the shelf in the kitchen cabinet. It wasn't the jar of mustard that couldn't be found while it sat on the second shelf in the refrigerator. This was a BIG, LARGE couch! How can this happen? Have you ever had an experience like this? Did you ever LOOK but not pay attention?

Our brains operate in strange ways at times. Our brain likes to identify things through comparison.

Whenever you are faced with a situation, your brain seeks to compare it with some past experiences. It doesn't like surprises. In the case of the couch, my brain had a picture of a couch in a horizontal position, the way you would normally expect to see a couch. When my eyes did not see what they expected to see(a horizontal couch) my brain communicated that there was no couch.

When I told myself that "I can't find the

Did you ever

look but not

pay attention?

couch," I gave my brain a command not to see the couch. In psychology, they call this a *schotoma*. When we look at things, in many instances, we see what we expect to see. If we don't, we need to have an explanation.

My brain immediately reasoned that the couch was gone and that somebody must have stolen it. This is an extreme example of how we can see and yet not see.

This is an obvious physical example of this idea. But, how many times do we do this in the course of a day and are not aware we are doing it?

By labeling something, we reduce the need to think and pay attention.

One way people do this regularly is by putting LABELS on people, things and places. By labeling something, we reduce the need to think and pay attention. Once you label somebody as lazy, an idiot, a liberal, a Republican, etc. then you don't pay attention to what they do or say, because you already know, or think you know them.

Labeling people involves the same type of situation as the missing couch. Once our brain locks in on something, it becomes difficult to change that perception. We can LOOK BUT WE AREN'T PAYING ATTENTION. We are not alert. The challenge becomes one of becoming more aware of how our perceptions, our prejudgments, OUR RULES of how things should be, can make it very difficult to LOOK AND PAY ATTENTION at the same time. What do you think?

109

What Is Love?

Love. Writers have written about it since the beginning of time. Musicians have sung about it. Poets have lamented about it. Yet, still to this day, we have great difficulty explaining what it is.

Johann Wolfgang Von Goethe suggested, "We are shaped and fashioned by what we love." What do you love?

If you ask people this question, you will be amazed at the responses you will get. People have a wide range of things that they love. They love their parents, their children, their husband or their wife, ice cream, pizza, their car, the movies, their pets, a certain hair style, and the list goes on and on.

There is something interesting when you begin to look at all the things people claim to love. In many instances, what people say they love are actually things that they LIKE. Somehow, in our fast paced, day-to day living, we have come to confuse LOVE with LIKE. The quality of a person's experiences can be directly impacted by the words they use to describe those experiences.

As a society, we have become too casual in our use of the term LOVE. Love is a very complicated and deeply empowering emotion. It is too important to just be casually thrown

Johann Wolfgang Von Goethe suggested, "We are shaped and fashioned by what we love."

about in describing such mundane things as pizza and ice cream. This may help to explain why so many people have such difficulty understanding what LOVE really is.

Love is not an easy thing. Real love is very hard. Gandhi suggested that, "A coward is incapable of exhibiting love; it is the prerogative of the brave." This is a very powerful thought. How much bravery is there in loving pizza or a dress or a movie?

It is our confusion in using language that often creates many of the difficulties we have in life. People too easily confuse LOVE with LIKE. LIKE is easy and changing. We move easily into and out of LIKE. It doesn't require much commitment or sacrifice. Just look at all the things you liked in the past that you don't like now. LIKE is merely a temporary preference for something that can easily be changed.

LOVE, on the other hand, requires a strong commitment. It can be painful. It is not something that we can easily move in an out of. It often requires sacrifice.

There are many different types of LOVE. There is the LOVE you have for your parents, your children, your husband or wife and the love you have for other people. The common denominator of LOVE is that it is a "giving" of something as opposed to a "getting." Sure, it is wonderful to receive LOVE and we all want and need LOVE. But, if the focus is just

" A coward

is incapable of

exhibiting love; it is

the prerogative

of the brave."

— Gandhi

112

on the receiving end, our chances of being loved can be significantly reduced.

To some people, LOVE exists as a noun, something to be acquired. In its true sense however, LOVE is really a verb, something you do. It is a great source of power and energy when it is given; given freely and without conditions. But this is LOVE in its most difficult form. LOVE today, seems to have many strings and conditions associated with it. The more conditions placed on it, the more difficult it is to both give and receive.

It is not possible to do justice to the meaning of LOVE in this brief writing. It may however, be helpful to you if you become a little more aware of the frequency and careless way you and others use the word LOVE to describe preferences for things. We can strengthen our understanding and the understanding others have about LOVE if we don't minimize the power that the word LOVE should have. Henry Wadsworth Longfellow expressed the belief that, "Love gives itself, it is not bought." What do you think?

You Are What You Think

"Circumstance does not make the man; it reveals him to himself." So wrote James Allen in his classic, 1904 book, "As A Man Thinketh." Allen's work is a powerful study of how an individual's thoughts shape his or her life.

Allen's belief that our external world is foundation on our inner world of thought is not unique to him. Other great thinkers throughout history have shared the same belief. What contributes to the value of Allen's work is its simplicity, common sense and brevity. These three factors all stem from the common characteristic that truth can always be stated simply.

A friend recently gifted me a copy of this powerful little book. It is a book I had read many years ago. But, reading it again, now, was a much more powerful experience for me.

It is often so easy to get caught up in the everyday challenges of life that we forget many of the simple common sense truths necessary for our happiness. We allow ourselves to get so caught up in the things of everyday life that we don't allow ourselves to circle our mental wagons to protect and re-capture our minds. Allen's little book is a tool to help us do this re-capturing.

> ' *Circumstance does not make the man; it reveals him to himself."*
>
> *— James Allen*

Allen's powerful metaphor of comparing a person's mind to a garden, vividly captures the power of our thoughts. When we realize that our thoughts can be compared to seeds planted in a garden, we better understand that whatever seeds(thoughts) we choose to plant will produce a harvest.

Each of us is the farmer of our mental garden. Each of us has the responsibility of keeping our mental gardens free from the weeds that can destroy and limit the beauty and happiness of our lives. Each of us is challenged to weed out those thoughts that are disruptive to our continual growth and development. In Allen's words, "...man is the causer(though nearly always unconsciously) of his circumstances, and that,whilst aiming at a good end, he is continually frustrating its accomplishment by encouraging thoughts and desires which cannot possibly harmonize with that end."

Doubt and fear are the great enemies of knowledge.

As we look around our world today, we find much confusion. Allen, writing in 1904, believed that people who have no central purpose in their lives, easily fall victim to petty worries, fears, troubles and self-pity. These mental seeds produce a harvest of failure, unhappiness and loss.To Allen, doubt and fear are the great enemies of knowledge. The person who feeds these enemies and who does not continually work to destroy them, undermines personal happiness and fulfillment.

116

In our society today, more and more people are becoming aware of how their eating habits effect their physical bodies. We are eating less fats and sugars. We are smoking less and drinking less alcohol. But, we have yet to act on strengthening our mental diets. We need to develop a better understanding of how what we feed our minds has greater power than what we feed our bodies. What do you think?

You And MTV

How familiar are you with the workings of MTV? Now you are probably familiar with the MTV that represents Music Television but, how familiar are you with the MTV that represents your own Mental Television? You see, all things are created twice; first in your mind and then in your physical, external environment. With this idea in mind, you become your own script writer, director, producer, musical composer and star in your own mental TV videos. How's that for a concept?

You have the power to choose the language, the lighting, the scenery, the costumes, the music and the story line for your own mental movies. The difficulty is that in most instances, you are not aware you are doing all these things. This is because they are happening at an unconscious level with great speed. What is most important to realize is that you have the power to change the pictures you are creating in your own mind. Everyone thinks in pictures. The pictures you create in your mind powerfully impact how you feel. And, in most instances, how you feel impacts how you behave.

Let's suppose, for an example, that there is someone that intimidates you. Maybe it's your boss, a co-worker or a neighbor. And let's further suppose that every time you think of this person, you become nervous. Think for a moment how you may be picturing this per-

Everyone

thinks

in pictures.

son in your mind. You are probably creating, without being aware of it, a mental movie that is contributing to your negative feelings.

Suppose you decide to re-direct this movie. Suppose you decide to outfit this person in a clown suit. And, since this is your own mental movie, you also decide to put a big red nose on this person and give them their own theme song. Maybe you would select a theme from one of your favorite cartoon characters or perhaps a circus theme. You could even choose to give this character a cartoon voice like Daffy Duck or Porky Pig. Hey, this is your own movie isn't it? You are in charge of production. Nobody else has to know what's going on in your mind.

Now, let's suppose that every time you think of this person in the future, you play this movie in your mind. You see this person in their costume, with their big red nose. You hear their cartoon theme song in the background as they approach you. Every time this person speaks, you hear the voice of Daffy Duck or Porky Pig. Do you think this new movie will help you to feel less intimidated when dealing with this person? I bet it does.

Have some fun with this idea. Activate your new role as a mental movie director. Let me know what happens. Remember, it's so easy to underestimate the powers of your mind. You have so much untapped creative mental potential just waiting to be activated. What do you think?

You have so much untapped creative mental potential just waiting to be activated.

The Power Of Newness

There is something exciting and magical about newness. Just think back to all the times in your life when you are excited about something new. It may have been a new tie, or a new dress, or maybe a new toy, new car, new shirt, or even a new house. The list can go on and on.

...the trap of newness is that it dosen't require much effort.

What is it that allows newness to produce this excitement? And how long does it last? I would like to suggest to you the excitement of newness is brought about by the expectations of change. The belief that this new thing, whatever it is, will produce some mystical, magical improvement in some aspect of our lives.

We all experience this. Think back to when you were going to school. Weren't you excited about your new clothes and your new notebooks? Didn't you resolve that at the start of every new school year, you were going to do much better than you did the year before? Didn't you really believe this? I know I did. But, what actually happened? Were your higher expectations realized? In most cases, I would suggest they weren't. Why?

Well, for the most part, newness is easy to achieve. How many times have you told yourself that if you only had that new dress, or that new computer, or that new car or that new

There can be no

meaningful

improvement without

an investment

in time,

effort and sacrifice.

piece of exercise equipment or that other teacher, then there would be a big improvement?

You see, the trap of newness is that it doesn't require much effort. It doesn't require the development of new habits. If newness is to bring about the changes that are expected, it must be accompanied by new habits of thought and new habits of behavior.

Developing new thinking and behavioral habits require hard work and great discipline. These are the things that are usually lacking when newness is present. It is much easier to buy new clothes, new notebooks and pens and go to a new school than it is to work to develop new attitudes, new study skills and to put in more time reading and doing homework. This is why the excitement of newness is so temporary and easy to achieve. And, this is why so many people mistakenly think that something new will easily bring them the improved results they are expecting.

There can be no meaningful improvement without an investment in time, effort and sacrifice. These are the qualities that will produce the changing results that we want.

I can remember years ago when I was a runner. I would go to the track and watch people with brand new, beautiful running outfits run around the track twice and then leave. The real runners would be wearing old, worn out sweat pants with holes, but they would just run and run and run.

Beware of the myth of newness. Too often, it will lead down the wrong path. Newness can give you a quick psychological jump-start, but as with most things in life, it is the follow-through that really counts. What do you think?

...it is the

follow-through

that really counts.

Have A Nice Day?

Have a nice day. How often are you told to do this in a given week? How do you react to this statement and what does this idea imply?

Besides its often robotic delivery, this statement suggests an interesting way of thinking. When someone tells you to have a nice day, it suggests that you, the individual, do not have much input as to whether your day will be nice or not. It reflects a kind of reactive approach to everyday experiences.

This reactive approach implies a style of thinking, that, when it is used, can limit a person's ability to tap their internal powers. People who regularly use this style of thinking, allow themselves to be easily influenced by the events of the day.

To suggest to someone that they have a nice day, implies that hopefully things will happen during the course of the day that will enable them to have a nice day.

Unfortunately, life doesn't work that way. Things happen in life everyday that you and I have no control over. You cannot control the weather, the days of the week, the traffic, what people say or do to you, and the list goes on and on. People who go through the challenges of daily life looking to have a nice day will, most often, be disappointed.

Things happen

in life everyday

that you and I

have no control over.

125

How many people allow the weather to impact the quality of their day? If the weather is good, they feel good. If it is bad, they feel bad. People who are working to be more effective and happier in the everyday life, seem to carry their own weather around with them. They realize that they can't really just HAVE a nice day, they have a responsibility to work at MAKING it a nice day. They realize that each person, has within themselves the potential power to make any day a nice day. Sure, if you happen to win the lottery, this would give you an added edge, but how often does that happen? There will always be some days where something happens that is well out of the ordinary. These are the exceptions.

Consider people who are easily impacted by what they hear on the early morning radio shows? How often have you heard some early morning radio personality telling you how bad the day was going to be because of either the weather or traffic or some other "condition" beyond your control? Would you believe that some people program the kind of day they are going to have before they even get out of bed in the morning simply because of what some one on the radio tells them?

How about the people who respond to the day of the week? You may know some of them. They are the ones who are unable to feel good because it's a Monday. They imply that one-seventh of their life will be wasted because they have to negotiate through Mondays. They

126

feel much better on Fridays. Suppose these people didn't know what day of the week it was, how would they know how to feel?

People who are more productive and happier carry their own weather, both physical and social, around with them. They in effect, create their own mental blue skies. They are not prisoners of what nature provides. They also don't allow themselves to become prisoners of the negative social weather that can easily be created by how others treat them. They understand that they can't just have a nice day, they have to MAKE it a nice day.

If you have developed the behavioral response of telling people to "have a nice day," why not re-think your response? What would happen if you began to tell people to MAKE IT A GREAT DAY!!!! What would happen if you began each day telling yourself to MAKE IT A GREAT DAY? It may help you to see the many opportunities you have every day to be more in control of your own weather forecast. What do you think?

People who are more productive and happier create their own weather

A Valentine's Tale

As he entered the bus, he was greeted by the smiles of a handful of passengers. He was a small, little man and he appeared to be in his early seventies.

He was carrying a dozen beautiful, long-stemmed, red roses. And, since this was Valentine's day, the passengers thought this to be a very cute sight.

As he sat down, a woman passenger commented to him, with a smile, that somebody is in for a very pleasant surprise. The old man politely smiled and nodded in silence.

As he sat quietly holding his roses, he couldn't help but notice the young man sitting across from him. The old man speculated the man to be in his early twenties. From the young man's appearance, the old man thought that the he may be having some financial difficulties.

As the bus continued on its journey, the old man noticed how the young man's eyes kept focusing on his roses.

Finally, the old man asked him if he had a girl friend. The young man answered yes, and said that he was on his way to see her now.

After a long thoughtful silence, the old man reached over to the young man and gave him the flowers. The young man politely declined the gesture. But, the old man was insistent. He told the young man that his wife would want his girl friend to have the roses, and that he was going to tell her what he had done. He was sure his wife would understand. The young man accepted the roses and thanked the old man. The two rode on in silence.

When the old man got off the bus, the young man's eyes followed him. He watched with a tear in his eye as the old man passed through the gates of the cemetery.

Valentine's day is but another opportunity to celebrate love. What do you think?

Creating The Future

Do you think that an idea, a small distinction, can change the quality of a person's life in a heartbeat? Do you think that at any given time, often when a person is not looking for it, they can have an experience that they value in such a way, it can change the course of their life?

Year end is traditionally a time when people and organizations look back over the past year and plan ahead for the new one. In looking back, we examine the things that we accomplished or didn't accomplish and then set some new goals as we move into the future.

All human beings need to have something to look forward to.

For some, rather than looking forward to the future, they seem stuck in the past. They continually focus on the way things used to be, and not on how things could be. In short, they do not have something to look forward to. All human beings need to have something to look forward to. The future should be an energizing force that drives us forward.

Consider the following idea: "the past does not determine the future." What do you think about this idea? Do you accept it as being valid? If you do, then this idea, if acted upon, can positively impact the rest of your life.

If you examine history, all success and accomplishment, whether individual, organizational or national, seems to be foundationed on this belief. Our pasts exist as memories; to be used from time to time to learn from and to enjoy. But, it is most important to understand that the past can only exist in our memories. It can not be relived. It serves as a basis or foundation for the future.

Unfortunately, many people live in their past. They don't seem to have a future, and this is sad because they deny themselves the excitement and growth that the future can provide.

Unfortunately, many people live in their past.

Some people believe that the past does determine the future. They believe that if they weren't able to do something in the past, they won't be able to do it in the future. This is definitely a disempowering and unresourceful belief. Just ask anyone who has achieved any long-term meaningful accomplishments. They will tell you that they believed that they could create their own future. If they were unsuccessful at something, they just re-thought what they had been doing and how they were doing it and came up with another plan or technique. They continued this process until they achieved their goal. They believed that the past did not determine the future.

On the other hand, past success does not determine future success. One of the principle causes for failure can prove to be success. Too often, success can lead to complacency. This complacency can lead to a false sense of security. The world is rapidly changing, and with change comes new challenges. To be-

The future is

where you

will be spending

the rest of your life.

lieve that just because you were successful in the past, you will be successful in the future is a belief that will ensure your future failure.

Each of us needs to be vigilant in our understanding that we can create our own future. We need to be looking forward to something, to be living in an environment of excited anticipation.

If you weren't successful in the past, that is no guarantee that you will be unsuccessful in the future. You may simply need a new belief like, the past does not determine the future and a new game plan. By continually acting on this belief, and by continually working to develop improved game plans you can create your own future.

Remember this works both ways, if you were successful in the past, that is no guarantee you will be successful in the future. You cannot live in the past. It is nice to visit the past through your memories, but you do not want to live there. The future is where you will be spending the rest of your life. Why not invest your energies in understanding and working on how you can better create the future you want? What do you think?

The Best Laid Plans Of...

How many of us

have a

master plan?

They move in strange and mysterious ways. They move quickly to the right, then to the left and again to the right, and then, they stop, for no apparent reason. They are living examples of chaos in motion. But don't be fooled by their confusing behavior. They have a plan. Who are they? They are the squirrels. And, Fall is their season.

Have you even taken the time to watch squirrels in action during the Fall months? As confusing as their behavior may appear, they do have a strategic plan. They are busily searching out food for the cold winter to come. They spend their time burying food so they will be able to survive the challenges of Winter. But alas, they do not have a very high success rate.

During the Winter months, squirrels will only find about 30% of the food that they buried in the Fall. And of that 30%, much of it was buried by other squirrels. You might say that all their frantic behavior, all their diligence and hard work during the Fall months will go unrewarded 70% of the time. You would be right. But, where would they be without all their efforts? Even though they will only be successful 30% of the time, without a master plan, they would not survive.

What about we humans? How many of us have a master plan? How many organizations have strategic, long-term plans? It has been suggested that the average person will spend more time planning a party or a vacation then their own life. Why?

Many people, and many organizations, believe that planning is not very effective. They believe in the Law of Accident rather than the Law of Cause and Affect. Since things change so rapidly, they believe that they really have no control of their environment so why should they waste time planning.

There is some truth to this belief. But the logic of it leaves a lot to be desired. Have you ever just gotten into your car without a plan or objective? Sounds like a pretty silly thing to do doesn't it? But, that's similar to going through life without some kind of master plan. This is true whether you are an individual or an organization.

What happens a lot, when you have a plan, is that things don't always go the way you had planned. And, when this happens, it is very easy to abandon the planning process on the reasoning that it doesn't work. Well, just as with our squirrel friends, while a plan may not be as successful as you would like, the question you should ask is, "Would I be better off with a plan or without a plan?" In just about every case, you would find that even though you didn't achieve what you wanted, you achieved more than you would have if you didn't have a plan. Try having a good party without a plan. You may get lucky once in a while, but for long-term consistency and success, you will need a plan.

If you haven't been successful at planning in the past, don't worry about it. Just think of those crazy squirrels. Their success rate is only 30%. One of the interesting things about planning is that you can become better at it the more you practice(accept for those crazy squirrels, their rate stays about the same). Another interesting thing to keep in mind is that you can alter your plans as circumstances change. You do not have to be locked into your plan. You can give yourself flexibility.

Why not give some thought to what you would like to be doing two or three or five or ten years from now? Make a plan and begin taking actions that will help you achieve your plan. Don't worry about achieving 100% success. Just think of those crazy squirrels. And remember, "Plan ahead. It wasn't raining when Noah started building the ark." What do you think?

" Plan ahead. It wasn't raining when Noah started building the ark. "

Practice, Practice, Practice

Pablo Casals, considered to be one of the greatest musicians of the twentieth century, was once asked by a reporter, "Why at the age of 86, do you still practice five and six hours a day?" His response, which I will never forget, was, "Because I think I'm getting better." Just think about his for a moment. Here is a man 86 years old, considered by many, at that time, to be the greatest cellist in the world, still practicing five and six hours a day merely because, he thought he was getting better.

This is a powerful insight into excellence. How often do we watch or read about people who are great at what they do and think that they have special talents that other people lack? Maybe you want to be able to do something like play the piano or the guitar or tennis or something else. Many people want to excel at something but, they don't want to invest the time and effort in what is needed for excellence, practice.

It seems many people look to negotiate the price of success. They want the easy way out. They don't want to go through the peaks and valleys and disciplined work of practice. It could be something as simple as staying in physical shape or eating well. Whatever it is, meaningful success in anything, cannot be achieved without continued practice.

It seems many people look to negotiate the price of success.

Thoreau suggested that, "What we do best or most perfectly is what we have most thoroughly learned by the longest practice, and at length it falls from us without our notice, as a leaf from a tree."

I am continually amazed at how many people view greatness as merely luck: people being in the right place at the right time, or, simply knowing the right people. Then there's the classic belief that great performers were just born with their skills. The fact is, all excellence is equally difficult.

When we see a great athlete, musician, businessman, cook, writer, actor or actress, we see a person in an arrival state. We don't see the countless hours of hard work, frustrations and disappointments that are part of the learning process called practice. We don't see that great athlete being the last one off the practice field. We don't see that struggling musician, investing hours, alone, working to develop and strengthen his fingers to be able to increase speed and dexterity. Nor do we see that great cook, alone in the kitchen, practicing. Or, how about that business person who just seems so lucky? We never see all the hard work, sleepless nights and monetary struggles that go into continued business success.

It is our dislike for practice that often prevents us for achieving the accomplishments we desire. We do not understand that it is practice

All excellence

is equally difficult.

140

that separates the excellent from the mediocre. It is continued practice that builds talent.
We are all born with great potential. It is
through practice that potential is actualized.
When we seek to short-cut success by refus-
ing to commit to practice, we are doing ourselves and society a dis-service.

Our modern society seems to be continually
encouraged to avoid excellence by its promises of fast, instant successes and its quest for
immediate gratification. These promises serve
to undercut and diminish the need for practice, and as a result, lead us in the opposite
direction of excellence.

We Americans are a very impatient people.
While this can be an asset at times, it can also
be a liability when it results in a reluctance to
invest the needed time, energy and commitment that produces excellence or what some
call MASTERY. This mastery or excellence
is ongoing. If you seek it, you must commit
to lifelong practice.

In a physical sense, excellence can be limited
by age. In other areas, limits become more
mental restraints. We find that most of the
resistance to practice is based on a lack of
mental toughness. This mental toughness requires that we give up our need for immediate
gratification and at the same time accept a
willingness to appear foolish or to make the
necessary mistakes that characterize this process called practice.

It is continued practice that builds talent.

141

When do we move out of the practice phase of life? I would suggest never. I suggest to you that life is a continual game involving continual practice. Just think again of Casals' response at the age of 86, "Because I think I'm getting better." What a powerful belief to have at that age. He lived his life of practice until the age of 97.

Perhaps Helen Keller summed it up best when she said, "We can do anything we want to do if we stick to it long enough." What do you think?

"We can do anything we want to do if we stick to it long enough."
— Helen Keller

Pride

What ever happened to the term pride? When was the last time you or some one else used the idea of pride in communication? How often do you hear this theme used in the course of your day, week, or month? I would suspect not too often.

Now, I am not going to attempt to give the definition of pride, I will leave that to you. What I would like to do is give you some ideas to think about related to pride.

Excellence is always the result of individuals or groups holding themselves to higher standards than others.

There is an interesting correlation between the diminishing use of the term pride and rising tide of social mischief and declining values we are experiencing in our society. Whether we focus on personal pride, family pride, organizational pride, neighborhood pride or national pride, pride is a concept that seems to have been lost in our every day lives. I am not looking at pride in its negative focus of snobbery or haughtiness, but in its empowering and dignity enhancing manner.

Any discussion of pride, would have to be linked to the notion of expectations and/or standards . Expectations, whether personal, societal or organizational, in many ways, have a powerful, contributing impact on performance or non-performance. When people individually or collectively hold themselves to low standards or expectations, it serves to diminish their sense of self-pride, self-respect and self-esteem.

143

Every human being wants to contribute to something meaningful.

There has been much written in recent years about how students and people in general, seem to be suffering from low self-esteem and that something needs to be done about this. I would suggest that it is not low self-esteem people are suffering from as much as it is a low level of expectations. We as a nation, in whatever category you would care to examine, have developed a mind-numbing mentality of low expectations. Low expectations, not only in ourselves but in what we demand and accept from each other.

The reason the term pride appears with less frequency in our every day conversations and in the media, is because to have pride, there needs to be high standards. High standards that cause individuals, families, organizations and even nations to stretch, to go the extra-mile. Excellence is always the result of individuals or groups holding themselves to higher standards than others.

What standards do you set for yourself in your every day activities? What standards do parents set for themselves and what standards do they help their children set? In education, what standards do educators set for themselves and to what standards do they elevate student performances?

In business, what standards do managers hold themselves to and what standards do they inspire their people to reach? What standards do national leaders strive to reach, and what inspiration do they provide for their people to elevate their own individual standards?

We don't have a crisis of low self-esteem, we have an absence of high standards in too many areas of our lives. This lack of meaningful high standards leads to a loss of pride and it is this loss in pride that contributes to low self-respect and low self-esteem.

Every human being wants to contribute to something meaningful. It is through this alignment with a purpose and a sense of contribution that makes life meaningful and exciting. We need people who will cause us to rise to the best that it is in each of us. But, more importantly, each of us must work to elevate our own personal standards and expectations so that we can elevate and build our own sense of personal pride, self- respect and self-esteem.

High standards bring with them responsibilities. When anyone or any system takes responsibility away from people, those people become dehumanized. In the words of philosopher and psychologist William James, "Compared to what we ought to be, we are only half awake. We are making use of only a small part of our physical and mental resources." Challenging and elevating our own personal standards will help us grow and will provide us with a higher level of self-respect, self-confidence and personal pride. What do you think?

> *"Compared to what we ought to be, we are only half awake. We are making use of only a small part of our physical and mental resources."*
> — *William James*

145

A Riddle For Life

*All life is
made up of
moments.*

Once upon a time, in a far off land, lived a beautiful Princess. And, as luck would have it, there also lived an evil Sorcerer. One day, the evil Sorcerer kidnapped the beautiful Princess and held her prisoner in his castle. The King, promised one-half of his kingdom to anyone who could rescue his daughter from this evil Sorcerer. There was however a risk. If you failed in your attempt to rescue the Princess, the Sorcerer would turn you into a frog.

Pretty soon, the land became inundated with frogs, for many brave adventurers attempted to rescue the Princess and failed. They found that when they arrived at the Sorcerer's castle, he gave them a riddle. He told them that if they could solve the riddle, they could have the Princess, if not, they would be sent home as frogs. This was the riddle he gave them: "There is something that exists for everyone exactly the same. This something moves commoners and kings in the same way. It touches everyone, yet no one can touch it." If you can bring this to me, said the Sorcerer, you can have the Princess.

Well, knight after knight, commoner after commoner all tried and failed to solve the riddle. One day, a young Prince arrived at the Sorcerer's castle. "I have solved your riddle!" the Prince yelled to the Sorcerer. "What is it?" asked the amused Sorcerer. It is, the

PRESENT MOMENT! RIGHT NOW! Everyone lives in it everywhere. It moves kings and commoners, it touches everyone, yet, no one can touch it, NOW! NOW is the answer to your riddle. On hearing this, the Sorcerer burst into flames and vanished. And with that, the Prince and the Princess lived happily for ever and ever.

If you think about it, all life is made up of moments. Minutes turn into hours. Hours turn into days. Days turn into weeks, weeks to months. Months turn into years and years turn into lifetimes. You know this, it is not some brilliant piece of insight.

What gradually happens as we go through life, is that we tend to forget these time relationships. We become easily focused on "someday," or "next week" or "next year." Or, we live in the past, carrying around the ghosts of our experiences. When we get annoyed, upset or angry, these temporary states can actually result from our inability to understand the power we can have by learning to "manage the moment."

As much as you would like to think otherwise, you only have control over the "present moment." You are not able to control the past or the future. Why not consider taking a look at life, on a moment by moment basis?

You are not able to control the past or the future.

What would happen if you worked on managing some of the tougher situations you face everyday on a moment to moment basis? If you were to become more focused on your momentary behavioral reactions to people and events, would this help you?

If you are on a diet, and just focused on better managing the moment when that dessert tray came around or the moment when you pass the bakery, would this help you? If you are working to stop smoking, if you better managed the moment when your desire to smoke was the strongest, would this help you? If your wife or husband or son or daughter was doing or saying something that in the past had really annoyed you, if you focused on managing that moment better, would this help you?

Too often we lose sight of the opportunities the "present moment" provides because we are either reliving the past in the "present moment," or we are attempting to predict the future by using the "present moment." In either case, we lose the opportunity of living through and dealing with, the actual "present moment."

By working to manage life's daily occurrences on a moment to moment basis, you can significantly improve your levels of effectiveness and happiness. What do you think?

Who Do You Think You Are?

Your answer to this question reflects the beliefs you carry around about yourself and helps form your self-concept. Psychological research suggests that it is a person's self-concept that determines how they think, how they behave and the way they perform in their everyday activities.

Our self-concept often controls how well we perform in many of our everyday activities.

We all carry around with us, a mental bag of beliefs about everything in our lives. Contained in this mental bag, is a smaller bag which contains particular beliefs about ourselves as a person and beliefs about how we should behave in the roles we perform in everyday. If we were to average all of these self-beliefs together, we would come up with a self-concept of ourselves.

This self-concept would answer the question, "Who do you think you are?" For example: What kind of parent are you? What kind of driver? What kind of employee? How well do you sing? How good of a cook are you? How good of a learner are you? The list can go on and on.

What we find, is that our self-concept often controls how well we perform in many of our everyday activities. If you have a self-concept of yourself as being a great cook, or a great mechanic, you will tend to perform up to that image. If on the other hand, you have a self-concept of yourself as a poor student or a poor driver, you will tend to perform down to that image.

Prescott Lecky, in his book, "Self Consistency: A Theory of Personality," suggests that people fail to succeed at things, not because of a lack of ability, but more often because of a poor self-concept they have about themselves related to the thing or activity they are performing.

When people reach into their mental bag of beliefs and pull out a set of negative pre-conceived beliefs or expectations about something they would like to do, they actually help to turn those beliefs and expectations into reality. Without realizing it, they are creating a kind of self-fulfilling prophecy. What will happen, in most instances, is that in order to prove themselves right, so that their beliefs will be validated, they will begin to look for all the factors that will support their negative beliefs and expectations. Their focus will be directed at the negatives, whether real or imagined.

Lecky's ideas support other research which suggests that an individual's self-concept is a much more powerful predictor of future performance than I.Q.

How can this information help you? Well, the next time you are going to do something that in the past you may not have been too successful at, check to see what beliefs you are pulling out of your little mental belief bag. Are these beliefs going to be helpful to you as you work on this activity? Are they going to empower you and put you into a resourceful state of mind? If not, where did they come from? What is the basis for these beliefs? What can you do to minimize or get rid of the negative self-concept you may have about yourself and this activity? What can you do to strengthen your self-concept as you work through this activity? By asking yourself these types of questions, you are engaging in a process that helps your brain to re-direct its focus so that it can develop and use more empowering information about you and your capabilities.

Why not begin to examine the self-concepts you are carrying around about yourself in some of the areas where you would like to improve your performance? Challenge the negative beliefs and expectations you are pulling from your little mental belief bag. The longer these beliefs go unchallenged, the more damage they can do. Remember the words of Henry Ford, "Whether you think you can do a thing or not, you are right." What do you think?

"Whether you think you can do a thing or not, you are right."

— Henry Ford

How's Your Self-Esteem These Days?

How's your self-esteem level these days? Have you had it checked lately? You may be a quart or two low.

Many years ago, I heard a speaker make the observation that at birth, each of us is born with a void, and that life is a continuous journey to fill that void. As we begin to fill this void, we begin to find inner peace. The void he was referring to was self-esteem, an appreciation of our self-worth.

The more a person looks for self-esteem externally, the more unhappiness they will generate for themselves.

According to Dr. Nathaniel Branden, a leader in the field of self-esteem, in order to better understand self-esteem, you will want to recognize that it has two components: a feeling of personal competence and a feeling of personal self-worth. Branden believes that self-esteem is an intimate experience. It resides in the core of your being. As such, it is an internal evaluation based on how you feel about yourself. It cannot be developed externally. It is not a function of what someone else thinks and feels about you. You can be loved and respected by others but you may not love and respect yourself. The more a person looks for self-esteem externally, the more unhappiness they will generate for themselves.

What is the basic source of our competence? It is our ability to think. In short, it is a mind that trusts itself. You might go as far as to say that our competence, our level of self-esteem is foundationed in self-love. This is not a narcissistic love, but rather a love of our own humanity, our own imperfection.

We have all made mistakes. We have all done things in the past that we regret; things that we may not have forgiven ourselves for. As a result, many people travel through life with feelings of inadequacy, insecurity, self-doubt and guilt. When a person focuses on their shortcomings and failures, they are focusing on the imperfect side of their human nature. What would happen if that person chose to focus on their strengths, talents and past accomplishments? What would happen if that person chose to focus on their untapped future human potential rather than on their past perceived human inadequacies? What impact would this change in focus have on their self-esteem?

At the heart of self-esteem is our own self-acceptance. If we are not able to accept ourselves, how can we acknowledge and appreciate the acceptances of others? Without our own self-acceptance, we will live under the shadow of our self-perception of being an imposter, unworthy of the acceptances of others.

...our level of self-esteem is foundation in self-love.

God didn't

create junk!

Growing greater self-esteem requires that you love yourself as you are, with all your strengths and shortcomings. It requires that you seek to strengthen your own internal self-evaluation process and not seek greater external evaluations. It requires that you focus more on your accomplishments and the good that is in you. As you do this, you will be able to focus on the good in others. You will in effect become a good finder. It is amazing how much better people feel when they focus on the positives rather than the negatives. Growth, productivity and happiness are based on positives, not negatives. When things get tough, and you begin to dump on yourself, always remember that, "God didn't create junk!"

Self-esteem is an inside job. You will not find greater self-confidence and greater self-respect outside of your own mind. Things will not bring you greater self-esteem. It is only through the controlled focus of your thinking that you will be able to fill the void of self-esteem that we all inherited at birth. What do you think?(For more ideas on self-esteem, see Dr. Nathaniel Branden's book, "How To Raise Your Self-Esteem.")

You Can Make A Difference

He didn't know what strange force had drawn him to the surf beating beach of Costabel. He somehow always believed he had a need to be there, but he didn't know why.

While he considered himself a teacher, he found that many of the perceptions he had drawn from his experiences frequently proved inadequate or betrayed. He was an anthropologist and an author. He had written eloquent works on science and human nature, yet he felt a certain emptiness. It was this feeling of emptiness that had drawn him to Costabel.

As he walked along the beach in the pre-dawn hours, he observed how the sea rejected its offspring; the unfortunate ones that could not fight their way back through the pounding surf that repeatedly threw them upon the shore.

In the distance, he noticed a human figure moving gracefully between the shore and the surf. As he approached this figure, he wondered what was generating this graceful, almost ballet type behavior. The figure proved to be that of a young man. His movements resulted from his picking up live starfish and throwing them beyond the beating surf, back into the sea.

What a strange behavior the author thought. He questioned the young man as to why he was doing this. The young man responded by saying that the sun would be up soon and the starfish would die. The author thought the young man mad to commit himself to this behavior. He suggested to the young man that the beach was full of starfish and that his actions could not possibly make a difference. The young man leaned over, picked up another starfish and as he hurled it beyond the roaring surf, stated that he had made a difference for that one.

Upon hearing the young man's response, the author walked away in amusement. What a ridiculous belief, and what an utter waste of time, he thought to himself.

But, as he continued his walk along the beach, he couldn't get the young man out of his mind. When he returned to his hotel room he continued to be bothered by this experience. He laid on his bed and thought about what he had just experienced. He thought about the other people he had seen on the beach at that time. They were the collectors of death. They were collecting the shelled, living creatures that the sea had rejected and they were boiling them to collect and sell their shells. It was only the star thrower who had focused on life.

He had always believed that death was the ultimate collector. Death was what couldn't be avoided. But, here on the beach of Costa-

> *"To laugh often and much; to win the respect of intelligent people: to appreciate beauty; to find the best in others; to leave the world a bit better, whether by a healthy child, a garden patch, or a redeemed social condition; to know even one life has breathed easier because you have lived, this is to have succeeded."*
> *— Ralph Waldo Emerson*

bel; here, through the actions of a stranger, he had learned something more powerful than anything else he had learned in his life. He had learned that each individual has the power to make a difference in the universe. Each individual, operating in their own little way, can choose to make a positive difference in the world.

The next morning, he went out in search of the star thrower. When he found him, he told him that he understood what he was doing, and the two of them spent the pre-dawn hours casting starfish back into the sea.

The author in this story was Loren Eisely, an American anthropologist and a writer of thought provoking books on the relationship of science and human nature. The ideas presented here are from his book, "The Unexpected Universe."

The lesson that can be drawn from this story is that individuals often underestimate their ability to make a difference because they believe they are only one person. They believe that their actions or their voice cannot be heard. But, the history of the world is written by individuals who believed they could make a difference.

You don't have to change the world. But, you can make a difference too! Just as with the star thrower, your influence can be small, but it can have an affect, it can contribute to the quality of life, in some way. In the words of Ralph Waldo Emerson, "To laugh often and much; to win the respect of intelligent people: to appreciate beauty; to find the best in others; to leave the world a bit better, whether by a healthy child, a garden patch, or a redeemed social condition; to know even one life has breathed easier because you have lived, this is to have succeeded." Each of us, in our own unique way, is a potential star thrower. What do you think?

Beware of the TCBs!

A few years ago, I had the distinct pleasure of attending a lecture by a very powerful speaker named Charlie Jones. Charlie travels around the world conducting management seminars for companies like IBM, Xerox, 3M, and other well known organizations. His mission is to get into the minds, spirits and hearts of individuals. In so doing, he hopes to help them improve their ability to make a tremendous life for themselves.

Hanging in my office is a poster I had made which captures one of Charlie's many thought provoking ideas. It states:

If you hang around achievers, you will be a better achiever; Hang around givers and you will be a better giver; Hang around thinkers and you will be a better thinker; But, hang around a bunch of thumb-sucking, complaining boneheads, and you will be a better thumb-sucking complaining bonehead.

As you can see, one of Charlie's great skills is his ability to use humor to stimulate thinking. Have you ever noticed how many thumb-sucking complaining boneheads there are in the world? Now, the unfortunate thing is that THEY don't see themselves as thumb-sucking complaining boneheads.

Which group

do you

associate with?

163

Which of these groups do you associate with? From which group do you get advice? Do you hang around with the givers? the thinkers? the achievers? or the TCBs?

Now you don't necessarily have to hang around these groups in a physical sense. How about people who are so-called experts? Or, how about people who operate in the fields of politics, medicine, science, law and education? Do you think there are any TCBs in these areas?

How about in the MEDIA? Some people think that just because they hear or read or see something in the media, it must be accurate and true. How many TCBs do you think are alive and well operating in the media?

What can you do to protect yourself from these TCBs? Well, you can begin by realizing that there will always be some one or some group looking to get into your mind. Every day, you can be guaranteed that somebody or some group is looking to SELL you something. It may be a product, a service or an idea. You cannot go through the day without being bombarded with messages directed at influencing you in some way.

What is important, is to recognize your responsibility to keep a vigilant guard at the gates of your mind. Be aware of what you are allowing to penetrate your thinking. Have you ever found yourself humming a commercial? This should be a warning to you that somehow, this message has gotten into your mind, and for the most part, you were not even aware of it.

Be aware of the thumb-sucking complaining boneheads. They are all around you. Watch and pay careful attention to where you are getting your information and ideas. Do not allow casual, easy access to your mind. Do not allow yourself the comfort of just one source of information. Do some research, check other sources. Don't allow other people to do your thinking for you, especially those TCBs. Remember the words of Claude McDonald, "Sometimes a majority simply means that all the fools are on the same side." What do you think?

"Sometimes a majority simply means that all the fools are on the same side."

— Claude McDonald

Time

Time has been called the great equalizer. Everyone has the same amount. It knows no boundaries. It is the same for the rich and the poor; the weak and the strong. It is a most valuable resource and yet no one seems to have enough of it.

Have you ever noticed how many people are always in a hurry. They seem to be busy running from point A to point B so that they can hurry and get to point C. But, where are they really going? It is our nature, particularly in New York, to always be in a hurry to go somewhere. I hope you find the ideas that follow thought provoking in putting TIME in an interesting perspective.

Time is an invention of man. It does not exist in the universe. Man developed the concept of time to meet HIS needs, and this serves to create his seemingly never ending challenge of managing it.

Time does not exist in nature. Nature doesn't have a calendar to tell it when Spring begins and ends or when Winter appears. To the best of our knowledge, God doesn't wear a watch.

The universe is estimated to be anywhere from 14 to 20 billion years old. Our galaxy, known as the Milky Way, is only one of the billions

Time is an

invention of man.

of star systems that are known to exist in the universe.

Astronomers estimate that our Milky Way Galaxy is about 100,000 light years wide and about 2,000 light years thick. Since light travels at the speed of 186,000 miles per second (in a vacum), the distance in one light year is about 5.9 trillion miles. I will leave the math to you and you can think about the distance in 100,000 light years. You might want to think about this the next time you travel on your favorite highway.

The Sun is estimated to be about 30,000 light years from the center of the universe.

The Sun is estimated to be about 30,000 light years from the center of the universe. To further add a little prospective to this, the Andromeda Galaxy is more than 2 million light years away from ours.

The Earth spins around its axis in New York, at the rate of 500 mph. At the equator, it spins at about 1,000 mph. It travels around the sun at 18 miles a second. With these ideas in mind, how does man's invention of the 24 hour day have any meaning in the universe?

Don't misunderstand me, I am not suggesting that time is not important. What I am suggesting is that perhaps we should take a good look at how we are spending our time.

In today's world, there is a high premium placed on speed. We have fast food, fast cars,

"There is

more to life than

increasing its speed."

— Gandhi

fast computers, and the list goes on and on. But, in our quest for speed, what are we giving up? Gandhi captured this idea quite well when it stated, "There is more to life than increasing its speed."

What is most important to you in life? How much of your time do you invest in this? Yes, invest, not spend. You see for us humans, time is a limited resource. Unlike the universe, which exists without time limits, our time is limited. It is a most precious resource and rather than just spending time, we need to view it as a scarce resource that needs to be invested, a resource that should give us a return. This return, should not be continually measured in economic terms but should be measured also in psychological ones.

When was the last time you took a long, slow walk through the woods, or just sat alone at the ocean and watched the power of nature at work? When was the last time you listened to snow falling or watched the majesty of the sun rise or set? How much time do you invest with your children and your family?

It is so easy to get caught up in the speed of life and to lose sight of the things that are most important. I find myself falling into this time trap too easily. It is most important for all of us to continually ask ourselves the question, "What's the most important to us in life?" We can then examine how much of our time we are devoting to the areas in our life we most value. By developing this habit of asking this question, we will be in a better position to invest our most precious resource of time in better and more empowering ways. What do you think?

Great Teaching

What does a teacher do? The words teacher and educator are used frequently to describe roles that people move in and out of at various times. But what is the role of the professional teacher?

As with any role, a person is not their role but simply generates a certain set of behaviors that fits their role. Great actors and actresses are great because they get us to believe that they are actually the person they are portraying. They assume both the verbal and non-verbal modes of communication that support their roles. But, what about the great teacher? What role does he or she perform in? What is their mission?

Great teachers do more than teach. They inspire. They motivate. They uplift. They elevate. They exhort. They get us to see ourselves not as we are, but as we can be. They transform us beyond our limiting self-beliefs and self-doubts. They enable us to see ourselves and the world in a new, more empowering way.

How do they do this? They start with a different belief system than most other teachers. They understand that beliefs are merely filters we use to process information. When we experience something, our brains continually ask, What does this mean? In the classroom,

Great teachers

do more

than teach.

a teacher asks this question repeatedly. The response gotten, determines the teacher's re-action to any given situation.

Great teachers do not seek to blame students for non-performance. They do not believe that their students are basically lazy and unmoti-vated. They do not believe that their students are not smart enough to do the work.

Great teachers go beyond the present state of affairs. They see students, not as they are, but as they can be. Rather than finding fault, they work to transform student beliefs through a disciplined environment of positive and en-couraging feedback. They exhibit behavior beyond the role of the average teacher. They exhibit behavior that communicates they are a friend, someone who really cares about their students and their performance.

Great teachers challenge their students and don't let them off the hook of personal respon-sibility. They work to strengthen their stu-dents' understanding for the importance of assuming personal responsibility for their ac-tions. They do not accept excuses for their students' poor performance. Great teachers recognize that excuses can simply reflect a person's lack of faith in their own power. They also believe that they are no better than the students they teach. Great teachers see them-

... excuses can simply reflect a person's lack of faith in their own power.

172

selves as performing in the roles of a learner and a student, just as their students do. Rather than talking down and at students, they talk to and with students.

In Latin, the word educate means "to draw out of." Some teachers believe that educating means to put into. It is this belief that can serve to reduce teaching effectiveness because it assumes that teaching is one-sided. In reality, can you really teach somebody? If you think about it, no one can teach anybody anything. All you can do is create an environment to help someone teach themselves

If teachers believe that to be effective, they just have to put information into their students, are they really teaching or are they providing a quick-fix education? Are they altering and elevating the self-beliefs of their students or are they developing student dependency on the teacher as the real source of learning? Are they really helping students learn how to learn or, are they just shoving in facts and information?

Transformational teaching builds a foundation for continued learning. It develops in students an improved belief system about their capabilities. It works to create a positive disciplined learning environment that challenges students to rise above mediocre performance.

"Who dares to teach,

must never

cease to learn."

— John Dana,

The challenge for education in the 21st century is one of creating an environment that stimulates and rewards the personal growth, learning and recognition of its teachers.

It challenges the teacher, to continually work to learn and to improve his or her own performance and skills.

It seems that some teachers stop learning. They stop growing. When teachers are not growing and learning, students are not growing and learning and this can contribute to a lack of excitement and enthusiasm in the classroom.

It can be argued that there are two basic mental states in life; growth and death. If we are not growing mentally, we are dying. There is no middle ground. There is no status quo.

Great teachers are continually challenging themselves to develop new and improved mental distinctions that will help them grow and improve their classroom performance and their own learning.

The challenge for education in the 21st century is one of creating an environment that stimulates and rewards the personal growth, learning and recognition of its teachers. Learning not just in the sense of subject knowledge, but learning that challenges teachers to develop more empowering beliefs not only about themselves but about their students and their profession. This learning works to strengthen the ability to see beyond today; to see what can be in the future; to enhance the powers of positive vision. In the words of John Dana, "Who dares to teach, must never cease to learn." What do you think?

The Ultimate Power

Vaclav Havel(Vahts'-lahv Hah'-vul) is not a household name in America, but it should be. In a world hungry for great leaders, Vaclav Havel deserves to be considered one. He is a Czech playwright and he is an activist for human rights. He is the elected president of the Czech Republic. On July 4, 1994, he was awarded the Philadelphia Liberty Medal. His acceptance speech, on that occasion, contained some powerful thoughts on the current state of our modern world and its future prospects.

Our experiences seem chaotic, disconnected and confusing.

He began with a brief review of world history and pointed out periods when values underwent fundamental shifts. He singled out the Hellenistic period, the Middle Ages and the Renaissance. He suggested that the common denominator of these transitional periods was a mixing and blending of cultures and a parallelism of intellectual and spiritual worlds. During these periods, value systems collapsed and new meaning was gradually developed by the connection of different elements.

In looking at today's world, Havel believes that through the developments of science and technology, our physical existence has been made easier in many ways. But he cautions, while our physical existence has been made easier, we do not know exactly what to do with ourselves. There are experts who can explain anything in our objective world to us, yet we, as individuals, understand our own lives less and less. Our experiences seem chaotic, disconnected and confusing. Our civilization, with its political and social focuses, only touches the surface of our lives.

In Havel's view, science has developed an unconditioned faith in an objective reality. It fosters a belief in its ability to do anything from space travel to biological engineering. And, while we are able to understand our human organs, their functions and their biochemical reactions, we lack the understanding of the spirit, purpose and meaning of the system that they create together. We are at a loss in explaining our own individual self, our own individual uniqueness. Science in its quest for universal laws, cannot explain uniqueness. To expect science to explain and to answer the interconnectedness of each of us to the universe and at the same time explain individual uniqueness goes beyond scientific boundaries.

He goes on to state that, "The abyss between the rational and the spiritual, the external and the internal, the objective and the subjective, the technical and the moral, the universal and the unique, constantly grows wider." Something is missing. He believes that what is missing is the common denominator that unites us all. When people believe that cultures can be united through some technical means they po-

We are at a loss in explaining our own individual self, our own individual uniqueness

176

What is missing is the common denominator that unites us all.

sition themselves for failure. To believe, as some do, that through some combination of political and diplomatic methods we can create some new organizational structure that will fill the voids existing in the world will also lead to failure.

The controversial belief that Havel ultimately proclaimed is that we need to recognize the existence of a Higher Authority than man himself. In his words, "We are not at all just an accidental anomaly, the microscopic caprice of a tiny particle whirling in the endless depths of the universe, we are mirrored in it, just as the entire evolution of the universe is mirrored in us."

Havel ended his ideas stating that, "The Declaration of Independence, adopted two hundred and eighteen years ago...states that the Creator gave man the right to liberty. It seems man can realize that liberty only if he does not forget the One who endowed him with it."

What gives Havel's ideas and beliefs such power is that unlike some American thinkers and writers, his thinking and writings have had advantages that they have not had. Havel has the reality based experience of living in oppression. Under the Communist rule of Czechoslovakia(1948-1989), not only were his writings banned, but he was imprisoned three times and he endured state punishment for the expression of his ideas. His experiences strengthened his belief that ultimate power is derived from the people. And, that while any one person or group may hold power, this power will be of a temporary nature if it does not represent the will of the people governed. This is why he is a great believer in democracy.

Havel is leading his people and their newly formed country into the 21st century, foundation on democracy and a belief in the Creator. Wasn't this also the foundation for the birth of our own country? What happened? How have we managed to lose sight of the beliefs and behaviors that made us the greatest country in the world? How have we gotten to the point in our history where if a teacher in school mentioned the word God, they can be threatened with dismissal? What would Mr. Havel say about this? We each have a lot of work to do in order to restore some of the key values that have been lost in our country. What do you think?

The Comparison Trap

Do you ever find yourself caught in the comparison trap? This is the trap where you compare yourself to other people. It is a trap that is very easy to fall into. How do you really benefit by doing this?

A wise man once observed that one of the principle causes of unhappiness in life is comparison. We humans are always comparing something to something else. We compare this restaurant to that restaurant; this school to that school; this child to that child; this company to that company; this person to that person; and on and on.

Why? Why do we have such a strong need to make these comparisons? Why can't we accept the uniqueness of people and things more, without having to make comparisons.

John Wooden was one of the greatest coaches of all time. He is the only man ever to be enshrined in the basketball Hall of Fame as both a player and a coach. He coached the UCLA basketball team for 27 years and his teams never had a losing season. In his last 12 years of coaching, his teams won 10 national championships, seven of them in a row, and he holds the record for the longest winning streak in college basketball, 88 games in a row(spanning 4 seasons).

One of the

principle causes

of unhappiness

in life

is comparison.

Success was from

the peace of mind

that resulted from

knowing that you did

your best.

With all of his success in winning, it is amazing to know that he never used the word winning with his teams. Rather than focusing on winning, he would tell his players that when the game was over, he wanted them to each be able to hold up their heads in pride, knowing that they each gave the best effort they were able to give. If they did that, the score didn't matter.

Wooden didn't want his players to compare themselves to any other players. He believed that the only valid comparisons occurred when individuals compared their own personal accomplishments with their own potential for accomplishment. In that way, an individual's true competition was with himself, and not with someone else.

Success to Wooden, was not in outscoring your competition. Success was from the peace of mind that resulted from knowing that you did your best. And that, he believed, is something that can only come from inside a person. It cannot come from someone or something external. True success becomes something that each individual must determine for themselves You can fool the outside world, but you can't fool yourself.

Wooden stated that, "You should never try to be better than someone else. But, you should never cease to be the best you could be." He instilled in his players a desire to never be satisfied with the past or the present, but to always be working to improve.

180

"You should never try

to be better than

someone else. But, you

should never

cease to be the best

you could be."

— John Wooden

He believed that to continue to be successful, one has to continually focus on the future.

So, while comparisons can be an interesting exercise in generating a sharing of opinions, the only meaningful comparisons are those you do against yourself and your potential. In the end, it doesn't matter how good somebody else is. That comparison doesn't make you any better or any worse. And, it doesn't matter what the outside world tells you. You are the only one who really knows what you have done. You are the only one who knows if your efforts are stretching you towards your potential. What do you think?

Where Are The Heros?

He never made the cover of Time magazine. And, you would never find his picture in Gentleman's Quarterly; he only owned one suit. You would never read about him in the newspaper. He never had a street named after him or a monument made in his honor.

He didn't have a PhD. In fact, he never graduated high school. He didn't own a business and he wasn't a politician. But, there was one thing that he was; he was a hero.

Today, more and more people are looking for heros.

Today, more and more people are looking for heros. Someone to lead them through the everyday, seemingly growing, challenges of life.

As the world seems to grow more and more complex, it becomes difficult to find real heros. There is a great temptation to look for them in the wrong places.

What is a hero? A hero is someone who demonstrates courage. Some one who acts inspite of fear. Someone who characterizes integrity, love and trust. A hero is someone who possesses great strength and at the same time great gentleness.

Most heros don't want to be heros. They don't

Quiet heros are

common people

with uncommon spirits.

see themselves as heros. Too often, we don't recognize our heros because we look for them in the wrong places.

Who was this hero who never made the cover of Time magazine? He was my father. In a way, he was like millions of other fathers throughout our nation. He belonged to a very special group of heros. A group I call, the quiet heros.

Quiet heros are common people with uncommon spirits. My father didn't know he was a hero. I never told him. He didn't know how his everyday example impacted my life.

This country was built by quiet heros. These are the people you never read about in the newspapers and the history books. Quiet heros live their lives with courage, integrity, loyalty and compassion. A quiet hero's spirit lives on long after they are gone. A hero's spirit never dies. It lives on in the minds, hearts and actions of those who knew them. A hero leaves behind the challenge of seeing to it that their spirit lives on.

When we look for heros, it is very easy to overlook those around us. This essay is dedicated to my father who, in every sense, was a quiet hero. It is also dedicated to the millions of other fathers who have gone before him, and to those living today. They are also part of this special group of quiet heros.

I believe that the worth of any nation can be examined by looking at the people that nation labels as its heros.   What do you think?

Suggested Readings

Allen, James: As A Man Thinketh. New York, Peter Pauper Press, 1948

Bennett, William: The Book of Virtues. New York, Simon & Shuster, 1993

Benson, Herbert: The Mind/Body Effect. New York, Berkley, 1980

Branden, Nathaniel: How To Raise Your Self-Esteem. New York, Bantam Books, 1988

Buzan, Tony: Use Both Sides of Your Brain. New York, Plume, 1989

Carnegie, Dale: How To Win Friends And Influence People. Pocket Books, 1990

Chopra, Deepak: The Seven Spiritual Laws of Success. California, New World Library, 1994

_____: Ageless Body, Timeless Mind. Crown Pub Group, 1993

_____: Perfect Health. Crown Pub Group, 1991

_____: Quantum Healing. New York, Bantam, 1990

Covey, Stephen: The 7 Habits of Highly Effective People. New York, Fireside, 1989

de Bono, Edward: The Six Thinking Hats. Boston, Little Brown, 1985

Eisely, Loren: The Unexpected Universe. New York, Harvest Books, 1969

Frankl, Viktor: Man's Search For Meaning. New York, Touchstone, 1984

Gardner, Howard: Frames of Mind. New York, Basic, 1983

Handy, Charles: The Age of Unreason. Boston, HBS, 1989

Jones, Charlie: Life Is Tremendous. Illinois, Tyndale, 1987

Leckey, Prescott: Self-Consistency: A Theory of Personality. Island PR Pubs, 1994

McCay, James T.: The Management of Time. Reward, 1986

Peck, M. Scott: The Road Less Traveled. New York, Touchstone, 1978

Robbins, Anthony: Unlimited Power. New York, Fawcett, 1986

_____: Awaken The Giant Within. New York, Summit, 1991

Schwartz, David: The Magic of Thinking Big. New York, Fireside, 1965

von Oech, Roger: A Whack On The Side Of The Head. New York, Warner, 1983

Waitley, Denis: The Psychology of Winning. New York, Berkley, 1979

Wycoff, Joyce: Mindmapping. New York, Berkley, 1991